SPEAKING TO THE HEART
FROM FLICKER TO FLAME
VOLUME THREE

ISAIAH 55:11

APRIL S. YARBER

Speaking to the Heart Publishing © 2024

23052 Alicia Parkway, Suite H 132
Mission Viejo, California 92692

Speaking to the Heart from Flicker to Flame, Volume Three
Copywrite © 2024 by April Yarber-Berg

All rights reserved. Copywrite allowance for all contributing writers of this anthology. They may reprint or use their own personal stories in any/all other works at their discretion.

Book Cover design by Mercy M.
Edited by April S. Yarber- Berg
Creator, Compiler, Co-Author: April S. Yarber-Berg

Scripture quotations are from individual authors. As such, the versions of the Bibles are noted but not the specific publications. This publication contains scripture quoted from the English Standard Version, (ESV), the Revised Standard Version, (RSV), the New International Version, (NIV), the New King James Version, (NKJV), the New Living Translation, (NLT), the Common English Bible, the (CEB), Easy-to-Read Version, (ERV), and the King James Version, (KJV) using BibleGateway.com.

All rights reserved. No part of this book may be reproduced or transmitted in any form or by any means, electronic or mechanical, including photocopying, recording, or by any information storage and retrieval system, without written permission of the publisher. Unless by a contributor of this written work. Contributors retain all rights to their personal stories to use at their discretions.

Library of Congress Control Number 2 0 2 3 9 1 7 4 3 4

ISBN:(paperback) 978-1-73796735-4

ISBN:(e-book) 978-1-7379673-6-1

¹¹ And they overcame him by the blood of the Lamb, and by the word of their testimony; and they loved not their lives unto the death.

- (Revelation 12:11, KJV)

DEDICATION

To our beautiful Savior, the Lord Jesus Christ, whom all glory, honor, and praise belongs!!!

May you be praised in it all.

And to the contributors, I can't thank you enough for sharing your beautiful servant hearts. Your openness to sharing touches my life and allows me to see Jesus in it all. It fuels me to keep on writing and collecting these stories for generations to come. Thank you for collaborating with me to show others who Jesus is, and how He loves

He so loves us all!!

Jesus is…our survival. He is our salvation. He is our Lord. He is our hope. A message that is needed so desperately in our world today.

Our mission statement is the same that was given to the original twelve…We walk with the same purpose and prayerfully in the same confidence as they did. Placing our lives in Jesus and going out into the world, to tell of Him and His wonderful deeds. To spread the Gospel Good News and shine a light in the darkness that others can draw near to, cling to.. and trust in…

We want *everyone* to be saved.

Let us press on toward the upward call and run the race with our love for others shining bright and let His love lead us all home… *together.*

As always with love, April~

A Special Verse Prayer-

For all the courageous contributors who shared their personal experiences and opened their hearts to ours, and for those who walk boldly in this world honoring God's call on their lives…

Now may the God of peace—
  who brought up from the dead our Lord Jesus,
the great Shepherd of the sheep,
  and ratified an eternal covenant with his blood—
may he equip you with all you need
  for doing his will.
May he produce in you,
  through the power of Jesus Christ,
every good thing that is pleasing to him.
  All glory to him forever and ever! Amen.

-(Hebrews 13:20-21, NLT)

INTRODUCTION

And so another journey begins…

I'm so excited you're here, and ready to experience for yourself the wonderous workings of our Lord Jesus, discovering we are never outside of His Presence. We can overcome situations and find our purpose in confidence while staying soaked in His word (the Bible.) Having the *eyes of our hearts* enlightened by **His Spirit** within...

All these miraculous encounters with the *Divine Presence of Jesus* as He purposed. These encounters you are about to read through are not merely stories; they are reflections of our shared journey, and a testament to our Savior. As we are all created in the image of God, and so loved by Him. Our identities are only truthfully fulfilled when we can see ourselves through the Spiritual lens of His sight. So read on and discover for yourself as we experience in awe-inspiring amazement the different ways in which our Lord shows up. Meeting us right where we are. He knows our Hearts. This is all written for one purpose: to give **Glory to the Lord Jesus**. And to draw others near to Him. Because He loves you.. and offers you more than the world can give…

My hope is that you will find HIM front and center allowing you the encouragement that you need to keep pressing on.

My prayer is that you are led by His Spirit to the perfect story within these pages. May He use it to speak to your heart, allowing you to feel a deep connection with Him. As an experience tailored exactly to you and whatever you may be going through. And that within it you will receive a blessing which in turn will help you to build your faith, taking it from flicker to FLAME once again, and may it remain with you fanning your FAITH all the days of your life…

CONTENTS

April Yarber-Berg
GOD ALWAYS FULFILLS HIS PURPOSE

Page 14

Sharyn Hernandez
EVERYONE WHO CALLS ON HIS NAME

Page 29

Cassandra Logan
THANK GOD

Page 44

Mark A. Willis
MY LIFE GODS GOT PLANS FOR YOU

Page 49

April May Diaz
JESUS FOREVER CHANGED MY HEART

Page 59

Barbara E. Kompik
I HEAR ANGELS

Page 73

Janice Bobanis
THE BOLD PROCLAIMER

Page 80

Hans Jacob
A CHRIST FOLLOWERS LIFE

Page 107

Didier Kwizera
ALWAYS WITH THE LOVE OF JESUS

Page 113

Carl and Kay Redlin
THE GOOD LORD WATCHING OVER

Page 121

Bonnie McBride
ROSE, HIS GOOD LESSON

Page 125

Candy J. Beard
IT ONLY TOOK FIFTEEN YEARS

Page 138

Shirley Rainwater
NEW BEGINNINGS

Page 174

Nancy J. Stoll
WHY LORD WHY

Page 180

Sue Rakoczy
WALK BY FAITH

Page 196

Dawn Hoskins
FROM BROKEN TO BEAUTIFUL

Page 200

JESUS MESSIAH

Poet: April S. Berg[1]

In the glow of the night a star was shone, leading the wise men to our Savior. There He lay in the hay, as a baby in form, wrapped in swaddling clothes in the manger.

And on this eve hope was restored as someday He would conquer death and the grave. He would pay for our sins and atone with His blood with the purest of life which God gave.

Jesus, came to save the lost, His precious life would be the cost. So now we sing Hallelujah with joy, for the gift of us all, this miraculous call, was the life of this wonderful boy...

---

[1] Jesus Messiah, written by April Berg- 2024.

Jesus, fully God fully man, only some understand, He is our Lord and our King. Jesus the name we lift high, with our eyes to the sky, and the wonderful truth that He brings.

As we celebrate His birth, and His immeasurable worth, as the Messiah for one and for all. For those who seek find, with eyes opened in time, as we answer His beckoning call.

May the Lord's peace be with you, and may all that you do, be blessed with His miraculous love, and to all of my friends, we shall win in the end, as we join with the angels above.

Hallelujah !! and God Bless!!!

GOD ALWAYS FULFILLS HIS PURPOSE
April S. Yarber- Berg

During my life…

I've had so many supernatural encounters, I can say without a shadow of a doubt that my eyes were opened pretty much since birth. I've experienced more than my fair share of these beautiful happenings graced by Jesus. And am grateful to have been blessed enough to recognize my Saviors hand, even without words or guidance. It has always felt natural, like my heart was already tuned to His Presence, an innate quiet truth living within me all along.

But when your attuned to Jesus and the supernatural your also attuned to the enemy who cloaks himself and deceives …That caused me a lot of problems in my life. But this experience I'm about to share with you- although some may find it hard to believe, happened just the way it was supposed to, and all the Glory, Honor, and Praise belongs to the Lord Jesus for what He would use to save lives and completely heal my heart and change my life for the good.

I still remember the room I had as a child to this day… It had light purple walls and on the floor a dark and light mixed shag carpet, this was the seventies after all. Also in my room was a very cute-girly, matching white, bedroom set with a canopy bed- and on the comforter there was an array of a dark-haired ballerina (truth be told she scared me.) I was never excited to go to bed and really didn't like bedtime, but what child does? On this night, my mother called out to me and said it was time to go to sleep. It was a night just like any other, or so I thought. But this night would open up something inside me. In a profound, yet subtle way, it would turn me just one degree. Stirring something within the deepest part of my heart. Something that would not leave me.

I reluctantly climbed in bed and dozed off, the next thing I remember is a lady waking me up. She was beautiful with blonde hair, wearing a white dress, and she had wings. Could I be dreaming? I thought I could, but the next thing happened so quickly- without saying a word she grabbed my hand and we flew through my bedroom wall towards the backside of my house, except we didn't end up where we should have been. We should have then been in my backyard, but more peculiar we flew straight into the bedroom of a little boy. He was wearing light blue pajamas and had blonde hair. He was so sad. I remember him crying and digging his little face into the blankets. He had a wad of blanket and some stuffed animals held tightly in both his fists...

He kneeled by the side of his bed and I thought he might be praying but he was crying into the covers. The lady looked at me and conveyed something without saying a word. "Someday this little boy is going to need you. Remember this" ...

With that we suddenly flew back into my room and that was it.

When I awoke the next day I thought I had been visited by the tooth fairy. So strange yet I kept this memory with me and it would pop up all throughout my dating life. It wasn't until many years later as I recalled the story to someone, they mentioned that tooth fairies were probably small and more fairy-like, like the size of Tinkerbell. And then in that instant, this intense feeling opened up a weighty thought: Could she have been an angel? In that moment, the realization felt deeply profound. As to my heart, it was revealed that yes this *was* an angel.

I went on with my life and had several relationships. Yet in the background, there was always that memory hidden in my heart. Whenever something would trigger that remembrance It would cause me to pause, If I was dating someone when it happened I would ask them if they had blonde hair as a child. - I was always searching for the one who I was told about long ago.

My life went on, I had a couple of children. I was married for a couple years, but that didn't work out so we got divorced. Still there was no sign of this little boy.

Truth is by this time, I had completely forgotten about it.

I had a job at a hospital and was doing pretty good. I started going to church with one of my boyfriends. That relationship ended, but this time it was me who chose to say goodbye. Although he was the nicest man, something inside my heart just didn't feel right and wouldn't let me settle. However the good that came out of it was that I continued going to church on my own. I would learn more about Jesus and find myself falling in love with our Lord and Savior in a new and deeper way. Now I longed for more of Him. I continued to pray to Jesus often asking Him for a partner.

Someone mentioned to me that when you're asking the Lord for anything, you need to be specific. So on my break at work one day I decided to make a list of my dream man- with all the qualities and attributes I wanted in a partner. I prayed to the Lord about it, stuck it in my desk. and forgot about it.

As a single mother I was lonely and I longed for a companion, someone to call my own, so I kept dating. Right before I met my husband, I had been casually dating a guy when that memory came flooding in. I wondered if this could be him (the little boy)? This relationship never got much deeper than casual and ended, but some strange things began to happen. One night I was cleaning my room listening to music, I lit a candle and it began to burn into the shape of a heart. It caught my attention so much though, that I took a picture of it. Later when I studied the picture, I was amazed to see that the wick in the center of the heart looked like a man wearing a baseball cap. Far-fetched, maybe to some, but to me and my heart it was something deeper. There was a feeling attached to this experience I couldn't shake off. I felt it was a sign. As if someone or something was trying to get my attention reaching out from beyond the veil, seeking to remind me.. and prepare me for the time that was to come.

When I met my husband James, we met at a bar during the day. He was wearing a baseball cap and always does, even to this day. But I didn't pay much attention to that fact and didn't really put two and two together until much later. On this day James was standing outside with his friends on a patio and I heard him say He wanted to stand by me. We started talking and exchanged numbers. He was very handsome and had the most attractive voice. So we began dating, I found out during this time that James, although so nice and cute was an alcoholic and had been for several years.

I knew that the Lord wouldn't want me with an alcoholic because I drank too. So every day on my way to work I would pray that if James wasn't the man for me, the Lord would remove him with kindness, but if he was, then He (The Lord) would clean James up. After only three months of dating and without knowing anything about my morning prayers, James would announce he was ready to go to rehab and get sober. That shocked me. Although this was an *answer to my prayer,* it was still a bit scary because I didn't know what to expect, or if this new relationship would make it. I decided to stop drinking as well- to show James support..

The program was located in Prescott Arizona, so quite far away from where we were living in California. He would be gone for three months. I was nervous but there was nothing I could do except pray and give it to the Lord Jesus -as He would be my peace. He would be my courage and give me the confidence I needed to stand firm against the enemy's attacks on my mind. I would have daily battles with thoughts that "I wasn't good enough and that James didn't love me, we would never make it." But then something would happen and it would be countered by the Lord. Sometimes He would use people who had a word of encouragement to give at just the right moment. At other times it might be a song that both James and I loved that would come on just when I was feeling the worst, or a movie I would watch that had a similar theme to what I was going through would grab my attention and provide me hope through my tears.

Whatever this was, whatever was happening, I clearly could see – This was a secret knowledge that *God* used to keep my heart in the truth that James and I were meant to be *together.*

The first month James was gone was the hardest, as we had no contact at all. By the second month I received a letter from James, telling me that we could write back and forth. Here was *another answered prayer* of mine. I had watched the movie the Notebook several times, and always wanted someone to write me love letters like the character Noah did to Alley in the movie. Over the next couple months I received some of the most beautiful love letters I've ever received in my life, from my James. These were even better than the kind that I had dreamt about. I received a huge stack of mushy, unrequited love letters, just like in the movie.

When he got out of rehab we started attending church and got baptized together. While I was waiting for James to propose life went on. One day I was cleaning out my desk at work and when I pulled my hand back out of my drawer a tattered piece of worn-out folded paper fell to the floor. Can you guess what it was? Yep it was the list of my perfect dream man that I had made two years earlier. As I unfolded it and read it I was astonished. It was a perfect description of James.

Theres always a bit of suffering in the waiting, and I was waiting for a proposal. I know some of you ladies reading this can understand the frustration. After a few years I was seriously at my wits end. Regardless of my overwhelming feelings on this day, I still had to go to work. I was just feeling really frustrated so I went on a break and poured my heart out to the Lord. I told him if James didn't ask me to marry him soon I was going to end our relationship.

When I went back into work, I was told to go to a meeting which was being held in another building across the campus. Yay for me. Don't you just love feeling upset and having to be around more people? After the meeting I was walking outside heading back to my office when I heard a man call out to me, "He's going to stay with you." I looked over to see a little Asian man in a straw fishing hat. He was smiling at me. I asked him, "Are you talking to me?" He simply nodded yes and proceeded, "You call each other pet names. (which we did.) The man continued, "He is going to stay with you." I remembered my conversation with the Lord from earlier that day. I smiled because I felt like this was a message to be patient. I told the man how much I needed to hear that and that he made me happy. I asked him how he knew? but he did not respond. He just smiled back at me as I passed him. Thats when I asked him his name. He said it was Peter. I waved at him and walked by, when I turned back around to say again thank you Peter, he was gone. It was as if he disappeared into thin air. Could this have been another angel?

Because of that angel/man I was patient even more. Eventually my husband would ask me. Now we have been married since 2020, and both have been sober for eleven years.

Now here's the part of the story, that blows me away even more. My husband's step mother Karen began taking care of James' grandmother. Since his grandma is getting older and has a home with lots of things in it that she can't take care of anymore, Karen was given the task of clearing things out and giving things away to those who might want them. So she began cleaning out old pictures of the family and other keepsakes... She had called and said there were some collectables and old photographs she wanted to give James. She brought them over and gave them to me to pass along. As I looked at the photographs one of them blew my mind. There in my hands was a picture of the little boy I had seen many years ago in his room. In this picture James was wearing *the same* light blue pajamas and clutching those same stuffed animals while lying in his bed. I almost fell over and instantly I began to cry. James is, and was, the little boy who needed me- someday.

I wanted to know more about why he was crying, so I asked James if he would have any reason to be upset during the time that the picture was taken. He explained to me that his mother and father had been divorced for some time at this point, but neither of them could take care of him nor his sister. The year before this, they were living with their aunt on his mother's side. His mother, who had been in an abusive relationship, finally ended it. So to keep the kids safe and to give them more stability they went to live with their grandma and grandpa. James was so sad that he couldn't live with his parents. He was worried about his mother and was adjusting to new surroundings. Thats why he was crying and had all those stuffed animals around him for comfort. It all began to make sense. I don't think James would have gotten sober if it wasn't for our connection. He did need me. The angel was right. God's word never comes back void but always fulfills that which He purposed. Our meeting was a double blessing, because James got sober, so did I. So for my family and children this changed my life.

It's a wonderful life filled with Jesus, love, and sobriety. Don't get me wrong, we as a couple struggle at times to understand each other. It still takes work. But in this relationship we communicate and respect each other's opinions even if they differ from our own. We value and love each other, in ways that I have never experienced with any other partner. I now have a healthy relationship. I have no desire to drink. I am a better person for my children and now grandchildren. I needed James as much as he needed me. I thank the Lord for him. I am so grateful if it wasn't for my relationship with James, I wouldn't be where I am today.

The Lord really used all of this to minister to my heart, and lead me into becoming who He created me to be. I am now a Christian Author. Also something that I had felt when I was a child and forgotten.

Again the word of the Lord proves true He is faithful and loves us. His love healed me and then when I was ready He gave me my James. I wouldn't change any of it. Not even the heartbreaks. I am the person I was created to be and I am with the person God chose for me. Everything happens in Gods time and we can often see the dots connecting as to why- years later looking back. As you can see, it would not be until many years later that God revealed their true significance, in His divine way. He turned my flicker of doubt into a full flame of understanding, showing me the greater purpose behind this experience. James told me if it wasn't for me, he would have kept drinking and probably *wouldn't be alive* this day. Thankfully, God had other plans for us. Some of the things I have been shown haven't come to pass just yet but I know they will…

Be thee encouraged.

Scripture Share

⁶ But from the beginning of creation, God made them male and female. ⁷ Therefore a man shall leave his father and mother and hold fast to his wife, ⁸ and the two shall become one flesh. So they are no longer two but one flesh. ⁹ What therefore God has joined together, let not man separate

. -(Mark 10:6-9, ESV)

Encouragement

I know waiting on the fulfillment of a promise Jesus has placed in your heart can feel like wandering through a desert, looking for signs of rain. But take heart! God's Word assures us in **Isaiah 55:11**, *"so is my word that goes out from my mouth: It will not return to me empty, but will accomplish what I desire and achieve the purpose for which I sent it."*

Such a powerful reminder that God's promises are not idle words. When *He speaks, His Word* is alive, purposeful, and unstoppable. It carries His Divine intention and cannot fail.

If you're feeling weary in the waiting, remember that God's timing is perfect. He is working in ways you cannot see, preparing you and the circumstances for the fulfillment of His promise. The seed of His Word planted in your heart will grow, just as surely as the sun will rise.

Don't give up and don't give in. Remain steadfast, and stand firm. Hold on to hope, for the One who made the promise is faithful. Trust that His plan for you is far greater than you can imagine, and His purposes for your life are unfolding—even now, as you are reading this -Even now as you wait. Just lean into His Presence, and let Him strengthen you with His peace In due season, the promise He gave you will come to pass, bringing glory to His name, setting your faith ablaze, and delivering immense joy to your heart. Trust Him with it *all*, and watch what He does. God Bless you!

As always with love April

EVERYONE WHO CALLS ON HIS NAME
Sharyn Hernandez

At eight years old I was bouncing around and trying to do the twist at my nineteen-year-old sister's wedding.

It was a lavish Jewish wedding with all the trim. The Rabbi, canopy for the ceremony, yarmulkes galore, and plenty of pickled salmon to go around. Not to mention a few choruses of Hava Nagila. I was torn between enjoying the event while disliking her new hubby Steve. While he loved my sister, his other job was to endlessly tease and torment me. I never had a brother before, and this was new to me. And besides, he was taking my sister away. But over the years he would prove to be a strong support and advocate, especially when my own husband would die of cancer from being a 911 first responder.

We weren't a very religious family. There are four- sects of Judaism and we were considered reformed. Jews by tradition with some observance of a few holidays. But all Jews observe Yom Kippur, the day of atonement, by fasting for twenty-four hours to have their sins forgiven. My mother and I did this as dutiful jews right up until we moved to Staten Island after my father passed away. My sister thought it would be better if we lived closer to her family.

During her first trip to the apartment house's laundry room, my mom met a Christian woman who invited her to church claiming they loved the Jewish people. My mother, very lonely and willing to go anywhere with anyone who had a car, went. And came home "saved". Excitedly, she told me Jesus was Jewish. So I too went. And came home saved. I gave my entire life to my Jewish messiah.

That was many years ago. Time passed. We had our families to raise, weddings to attend, grandchildren to welcome. My sister and Steve retired, sold their home of fifty-five years and headed south to Florida into a retirement village. They had a gorgeous view of the lake from their family room, pools, and community. Not to mention perfect weather. And we all loved visiting them. It became the new family vacation hot spot.

Yes, they were set and their plans were coming to fulfillment. That is, until something terribly unplanned happened.

It was 2022, they had been living down south about eight months when Steve began having stomach issues. Constant indigestion, and terrible backache. He had spinal surgery the year before, so he naturally thought it was a flare up. But the Doctor could find no abnormalities in his spine. My sister noted that he had bouts of feeling sick and weak. Not to mention his belly was very bloated. She thought it was the cheese-danish he loved to snack on. But one day he had terrible belly pain and a trip to the ER, complete with all kinds of scans showed an advanced stage of stomach cancer. This was no cheese-danish. Shocked, the entire family rushed down. This was July.

When August came, he was not able to eat very much. I kept asking if I could come but my sister discouraged me saying it was too crowded. There were already too many family members in their two-bedroom house. She said she would let me know. So I waited.

About the early part of September, my niece Melissa had been keeping me posted about her dad's condition. With all tests coming back badly, it was obvious he was deteriorating. She said she didn't believe he'd live another month. I knew I'd have to go there soon. But it wasn't till she called me up and said that Steve had had two awful nights in which he saw horrible creatures in his hospital room that he could not discuss. He also related that a he kept seeing a dark figure standing at the foot of his hospital bed every night. I knew that his impending departure from this earth was near, and the forces of hell knew it too. Hovering and waiting to take another unsaved soul to their damnable destiny. With this, my daughter said, "Mom! You've got to get down there and pray for him!!" I flew down the next day.

My other niece Sheri picked me up from the airport and we drove straight to the hospital. The oncologist said Steve had gotten one dose of chemo and was sleeping it off. That actually felt hopeful. When we entered his room, I was met with the sight of a small man in bed wearing dark sunglasses and hooked up to an array of clicking and buzzing I.V. machines. I would never have known it was Steve except for his perpetual stoic expression. Only now he had good reason for it.

Everyone supposed he wanted the sunglasses so people would not see his sickly-looking expression. But truthfully, I knew he was trying to block out the visions he had been seeing. He kept a pink basin under his chin in case he had the need to vomit. A few days later he began to vomit blood. We hoped it was just the drugs breaking up the tumors. He could no longer eat, nor drink, as even the smallest amount would result in an agonizing twelve-hour bout of hiccups. So he was only allowed to swish some water in his mouth and apply chap stick to his lips. I couldn't imagine how thirsty he must have been.

The first few nights Melissa stayed overnight by his bedside. Because he needed constant help, the nurse's usual fifteen-minute check-ins weren't enough. Sheri also stayed. And to be sure, they were very exhausted. I kept hinting that we gals should go out for a bite elsewhere (the cold chicken fingers and soggy french-fries the hospital offered were not appetizing) or do something other than sit 8-12 hours in the hospital. But of course I was outvoted. Their patriarch was dying. So they hired an aid named Marlene to stay the nights with him. Twenty-dollars an hour and well worth it. Sweet. Full of joy. Insisting she never sleeps at night. Just lost her husband to covid the last-year. Sneaking suspicion there was a Christian lurking in there somewhere. Now we could ALL go back to the house to sleep. As if we could.

When I came the first day I managed to be alone at one point with him and Sheri. So I got my courage up and said that I heard that he had been seeing some unpleasant things. I told him I had kept my peace and respected his Jewish beliefs for forty-three years. But both myself and my mother had felt that Jesus was the Messiah for all people. I told him there was power in the name of Jesus and to remember his name. Then I openly rebuked any demonic beings, prayed for healing, and said, Amen. He didn't stop me. He just let me go on. I should mention my sister Joyce had sent me a text actually asking me for prayers, but specifically not to use the name of Jesus because it wasn't how we were raised. My niece had to get her out to the cafeteria so that I could pray freely.

My sister-in-law Cookie texted me out of the blue inquiring about Steve's health. I gave her an update and she was so happy to hear that I was able to pray over him. But even after, I had my lingering doubts. Doubts that my prayers reached heaven. Doubts that

Steve paid much mind to it. Doubts that it really did anything at all except accomplish what I had come there to do - just to pray over him. But Cookie shot me a wonderful text exclaiming that she whole heartedly believed my prayer hit the throne room and that God heard and Steve was going to be saved. But...I still had this...doubt. "Lord, I know you led me to pray. But just because you pray for someone doesn't mean anything. I need a sign. In all the years I've been a believer, I've never asked for one. But I'm asking you now for a supernatural sign that Steve will be with you. Not just an encouraging scripture, but something else. Something that I will recognize being from you".

Later that night, Sheri asked if I had gotten a photo she sent to me that her daughter took showing sky writing. It was the first day Steve entered the hospital. I assured her I never received it. She said it was taken upside down, but she recognized the word God in it. She re-sent it to me, and I reversed the photo to right side up. The photo revealed a clear blue sky with white lettering. "STEVE...U + GOD = (happy face emoji with spiked hair). WHAT!!!??? I screamed!! Remarkable! Praise God! I had my sign.

At the end of the week a hospice rep came to talk to us about end-of-life palliative care. "Well, if there's really nothing more that can be done", Steve said softly. I left the weeping room to take shelter down the hall in one of the waiting rooms. And lost it.

When he was transferred to hospice, we came after they had settled him in. The hallway was dimly lit and quiet. Very few visitors. No happy sounds. No buzzing machines. No balloons conveying get well wishes. No sir. People came there with only one purpose. They came to die.

Steve's friends all came to sort of say their goodbyes. One friend even drove twenty- hours straight from NY. When he entered his room, they gave each other one last brother to brother fist pump. The first night Joyce wanted to stay. She had dismissed Marlene since Steve was no longer in the hospital and the hospice staff was more attentive. But though he was receiving some pain medication, he still needed that extra assurance. The next morning my sister was drained and so, faithful Marlene was called upon once again. She showed up that evening announcing, "Hello Mr. Steve, I'm back!" He smiled.

After Melissa and I came back with food, we joined Sheri and my sister in the snack room. She mentioned that her dad was starting to say weird things. That didn't surprise me. I assumed it might have been the strong meds. But then she mentioned he kept yelling for help over and over. *That* was my cue. I ran into his room. Marlene stayed across the room, allowing us to gather around his bed. There he lay, greatly troubled. Wanting to bolt out of his bed. "Help me! Help me! No! No!! Help me! Help me!!"

Knowing just what was happening, I held his arm tightly. My sister kept trying to assure him she loved him and was there. I knew his cries went a lot deeper. He was transitioning. And probably being taunted by visitors from the dark side. At one point, he cried, "Eddie! Eddie! Eddie! Oh no!" Eddie was his best friend who had died a few months earlier. A sweet funny man. Good father, husband, and Grandpa. Now perhaps experiencing the consequences of dying without the mark of Christ on his life. Perhaps that's what Steve was seeing in the spirit. This all upset me so much. I thought God gave me my sign. What was this? Perhaps it was Satan's final attempt to claim Steve's soul. After all, he spent seventy-nine years unsaved.

It was time to leave for the night. If anything, we all felt assured that Marlene would be there. We kissed him good night and said we'd be back in the morning. But in his agitated state he didn't acknowledge. As we walked the hallway I signaled to Melissa I was going back in. I slipped into the darkened room, wrapped my arms around his head and spoke loudly into his ear. "STEVE!" He nodded and uttered, "Yeah". Say, *"JESUS SAVE ME! JESUS HELP ME! REMEMBER I TOLD YOU THERE IS POWER IN HIS NAME. YOU HAVE TO SHOUT IT! JESUS SAVE ME! JESUS HELP ME! JESUS SAVE ME! JESUS HELP ME!* And He will help you". With that Marlene gave me a wink as I headed for the door. It was all I could do.

The life changing call came at six-thirty in the morning. I heard the hysterics through my bedroom door. We all hugged and cried. Terrible news, how in the world does a strong head of the family get cancer so quickly and just die? We got ready and drove to hospice for the last time. In his bed, he lay there. Still. Blanket pulled up to his neck. Sheri kissed him. His wife whispered her last "I love you." Melissa closed his eyes. We all soberly walked

out. Just then, sweet Marlene quietly called me over to her and gave me the most incredible message I ever heard in my life.
"He listened to you!", she said excitedly. "He listened to you! He said, "JESUS SAVE ME! JESUS HELP ME!" Then he raised his arms up high and slowly lowered them. The rest of the night he was calm and quiet. Till he died".

I was OVERJOYED! He did it! He said His name! He said the name of Jesus! And the gates of hell could NOT prevail! Boy I'll tell ya,' it was hard to hide my smile walking out. Now for sure he knows who his Messiah is.

> *"Everyone who calls on the name of*
> *the Lord will be saved".*
> *-(Romans 10:13)*

Steve *did*. Hallelujah!

Over the years as I've faced various trials and circumstances, I eventually have turned to the Lord for help and insight. Unfortunately, later rather than sooner. After trying every possible avenue and exhausting any resource available to me, I would come up with a "game plan". But in the last few years, I finally have come to that place of giving it over to God sooner, rather than later. I decided I was going to "discuss" the variables of the situation and simply believe He was going to take care of the details. And to my amazement, He does. Every time. I know I should not really be all that amazed.

A favorite verse of mine comes from *Exodus 14:14. "The Lord will fight for you and you have only to be silent (still)."*

God pleads our case, provides for us, makes crooked paths straight. This always encourages me through every occurrence I may face. I need only to trust Him (even for unsaved loved ones). To surrender my struggle and worries to Him. What a relief to know He's already working on the situation - for me. In Him I can place my confidence, and relax!

Scripture Share
"Believe in the Lord Jesus and you will be saved - you and your household."

-(Acts16:31, ESV)

Encouragement

This scripture has always encouraged me to keep on believing and praying for my loved ones salvation. No matter what they may believe personally or whether or not they have received what I have tried to share about Jesus, it comes down to this. It's not about them. I can't put my trust or hope in their humanity. But my trust, hope, and confidence is in a God who is faithful to His word. He loves our loved ones even more than we can or do. Hold on to this and don't lose hope for them. Persevere in prayer no matter how long. Our Lord hears and knows.

Blessings, Sharyn

If you do not know Jesus as your Lord and Savior, and are ready to turn your life over to Him, just pray the prayer on the next page and you will be born again.[2] Then find yourself a bible believing church and walk with the Lord.

---

[2] *John 3:3 Jesus replied, "Very truly I tell you, no one can see the kingdom of God unless they are born again." (NIV)*

Dear Heavenly Father,

I believe that Jesus died for me. I believe that Jesus paid for my sins on the cross. I believe that Jesus rose from the dead. I ask you to forgive me of my sins. I ask you to wash me clean of all sin.

I put my faith and trust in Jesus as my only hope for living eternally with you in heaven.

I ask Jesus to be my Savior and my Lord. I want to live my life for Christ.

I understand that my salvation is not based on my works but on the sacrifice of Jesus on the cross.

Thank you for saving me!

Amen![3]

---

[3] This prayer was copied from the internet. The author's name of the prayer is unknown, but we would like to thank him, as we have used this prayer many times when leading people to Christ.

THANK GOD

Cassandra Logan

I want to share with you a personal chapter of my life—

A story of loss, grace, and the unmistakable presence of God's timing. Even in the midst of my grief, something beautiful happened. Something I now know was not by accident, but by divine design.

This is the story of the night my dad passed away...

My dad had been in the hospital for a couple weeks., when my best friend since kindergarten, Meghan, called me out of the blue. It was really late for me with the two-hour time difference between us. I was in bed, and normally I would let it go to voicemail, but I picked up the phone. I wouldn't say that my friend is the religious type, but she called to let me know that she tore her house apart looking for the rosary her grandma had left her.

She said she felt compelled to say a prayer for my dad but couldn't quite remember the words and needed my help. I helped her recite **The Lord's Prayer**. The next thing I know, my step mom is calling on the other line. I looked at the phone and I knew. I knew before I clicked over to the other line and heard her say the words *"He's gone."* I clicked back over to my friend. I couldn't get the words out past the lump in my throat. I felt like I couldn't breathe, but she knew too without me having to say a word. We sat on the phone until 5am praying and crying, laughing, and talking for hours about our friendship and all the special times we've had with our families.

God knew exactly who I *needed* in that moment.

The ONLY person on the planet that knew my dad the way that I did. The only person that grew up alongside me with so many of the same stories and memories of him. My person. My Mey. It's no coincidence that she called late that night and I thank God for her every day.

It was you see the exact moment when I was about to feel most alone, when the weight of my sorrow would otherwise seem unbearable, my best friend was there. Not by coincidence, but because God's timing is always perfect. I often wonder how it is that, at just the right moment, she reached out to me, offering her comfort, her prayers, and her presence. *In a way only He could orchestrate*, God knew exactly *who* I needed and when I needed them.

As I walked through the pain of losing my dad, I was reminded that God's love is not just in the blessings we see, but also in the people He places in our lives at the right time. My best friend was not just a shoulder to cry on. She was God's answer to my prayers, a tangible reminder that He is always with us, even in our darkest moments.

I've come to see that *God's* ways *are far greater* than our understanding.

His timing is perfect. He knows our hearts, our pain, and our needs better than we ever could. I am truly grateful for the people He has placed in my life to walk with me through seasons of joy and sorrow. And I am learning to trust that even in my deepest pain, He is working all things together for good.

Scripture Share

But seek first the kingdom of God and his righteousness, and all these things will be added to you.
-(Matthew 6:33, ESV)

Encouragement

To anyone who may be walking through their own seasons of loss or hardship, I want to remind you: God knows exactly what and who you need, and He will bring those into your life at just the right time. His love and provision are far-reaching, and His timing is always, always perfect. Thank you for allowing me to share this part of my journey with you. I pray that it encourages you to trust in God's timing and the people He sends into your life to bring you peace and healing.

Held In His Perfect Peace. -

Cassie

✝

MY LIFE GODS GOT PLANS FOR YOU
Pastor Mark A. Willis

This is a story to assist people in the best way I feel like I can. How can I be of help? You may wonder who I am? ..

Well, to let you know in short., recently I was involved in a pretty severe car accident. Basically everything I had was taken from me. Am I upset.? Sometimes, but I serve a God that has everything under His control. You see, He already knows what's going to happen to me and also you. *Genesis 28:15* says, *Behold, I am with you, and will keep you wherever you go, and I will bring you back into the land I have promised.; For I will not leave you till I have done that which I promised.*

You may not know the plans He has for you, but He does have them. All that He asks you to do is serve and obey Him. There may be times when it's difficult, it might seem almost impossible to do., But with God on your side, all things are possible.

Matthew 19:26, KJV- *But Jesus beheld them., and said unto them., With men this is impossible; But with God all things are possible.*

The Apostle Paul didn't know what was going to happen to him, but he continued to preach and although he ended up in prison he chose to serve God anyways... That's the kind of faith and trust that has to be kept at the forefront of our lives, no matter how dark the storm.

My Early Years...

I never knew my birth father... My mother who served in the Army became pregnant with me during the Korean war. After she was discharged she came to Arizona, and before I was born married my step-father. She was married to him for about ten years. The marriage, which had its ups and downs unfortunately didn't survive. Following her divorce she moved us in with her boyfriend. When they broke up we moved to a new house. I was glad when that happened because while living there with her boyfriend he molested me. We lived in our new home for about six months when my mother killed herself. I believe it was partially due to the pain she felt because she found out.

After her death I moved back in with my step father for about a year. From there I moved into my aunts home in Michigan. I lived with her about four years. Thankfully, that's where I was first introduced to Jesus Christ and accepted Him as my Lord and Savior. I was baptized in the river Au Gres. I wrote a song there and sang it for the church…

>One day as I was walking
>Down a very lonely path.
>I saw my Lord and Savior
>In His heaven home at last.
>I heard Him say out loud to me
>My good and faithful servant
>I'm glad you gave your life to me,
>Now I will come and set you free.
>So come along one and all
>I have a story for you all
>Of a God who saved us by His grace
>And in Heaven has prepared a place.
>Not just for me but also you
>All He asks that you do
>Is serve Him Oh so faithfully
>And live each day prayerfully.

My life was never easy. There seemed to be a lot of hard things but now I had Jesus and He would eventually help me heal.

From there my life just kept on moving. We left Michigan moving first to Arizona then to Florida. My life would now take another turn as I moved back to Arizona with another Aunt and Uncle. I was in high school by this time. I wasn't attending church anymore and got involved with drugs. I ended up getting arrested because I sold an ounce and a half of cocaine to an undercover officer. Listen drugs, may be fun for a season, but they have a cost. They are not worth it. I'm glad I got caught, it could have been worse. That trouble caused me to wake up and I felt prompted to find a church and reconnect with God. I like to say that I found Him again. But in actuality He never left me. He was waiting patiently for me to repent and turn again to Him.

Jesus never holds anything against us. He received me with open arms. He forgave me of all the bad stuff that I had been involved with. He will forgive you as well, if you simply ask Him to, then make Him Lord of your life.

Nothing is too difficult for God…

I woke up one morning and everything that I had was gone. Why?? I had been a pastor at a church for about a year. I went to Bible college. First in Arizona where I got my associate degree. Then moved to Minnesota and got my bachelor's degree in Cross Cultural Ministries. For just about three years I was a youth pastor in Wisconsin. I have been on many mission trips. It seemed as if everything was going well., well as good as could be expected.

I then moved back to Arizona and found a job as a Pastor there. The church I was at was going OK. I had been there for just about a year. We were in the process of closing down. It just wasn't seeming to make it. Yes, It was a small church. We did have our problems., What church doesn't? I was in the process of looking for another church. So I decided to attended a Ministers Renewal Meeting. While there I met another pastor named Joe Pangio, who I never met before. We spoke a bit. That's when he shared with me that he had a vision, and *I was in it.*

THE VISION

He was walking down a seashore, and he had a gun in his hands. I was beside him and we were friends. We walked along the beach and on the other side was a forest. He left me because he saw an island just offshore. In the center of the island there was a large statue of a snake. In the shape of an S. He shot the statue when it came to life and fell in the water. He saw that there were thousands of other snakes covering it. They were protecting it. So he returned to the shore where I was. He saw that I was lying down. He then saw the snake coming out of the water as well, and it tried to swallow me. Then he came out of the vision.

From this I received (Proverbs 6:30-31), Anything Satan tries to destroy but fails at, he owes you seven times over.

> *[30] People do not despise a thief if he steals*
> *to satisfy his appetite when he is hungry,*
> *[31] but if he is caught, he will pay sevenfold;*
> *he will give all the goods of his house.*
> *-(Proverbs 6:30-31, ESV)*

After the Ministers Renewal Retreat was over, Joe asked me if I could give him a ride to the airport. I was happy to oblige. We got in my car and headed out. But on the way we were involved in a pretty severe car accident. We hit some ice on the road, lost control, another car hit us, and we went over a cliff. My car was totaled. I suffered some brain damage. My left leg was broken over forty-times. oh yeah, I was also in a coma for two months. When I came out of the coma for a couple days, I was able to talk. Then the brain damaged set in and I could no longer form words. Your probably wondering what happened to my passenger Joe, well by the grace of God he only suffered a few minor bruises.

Initially, the doctors said I'd *never* walk again or regain my speech. They gave me a pretty poor outlook. They didn't think I'd ever amount to much. About that time another Pastor friend of mine, Richard Brown., came to see me and he said, "Now we'll see what God has to say." You see I serve a big God. He has plans for me and for you. You just need to give Him a chance to work both *in* and *through* you. You only need to be open to Him.

I spent three years in rehabilitation. First at a hospital, then with a place called Gentiva. It's a place that specializes in rehabilitation for people that have had strokes and brain injuries like I have. I worked with them for about six months, then I did other things. There's still a lot that I need to do, I just need to keep in mind that

God is in control. Even when I feel like He's not interested. Just like Job did., I need to keep praising Him.

> [11] *My foot has held fast to his steps;*
> *I have kept his way and have not turned aside.*
>
> [12] *I have not departed from the commandment of his lips; I have treasured the words of his mouth more than my portion of food.*
>
> [13] *But he is unchangeable, and who can turn him back? What he desires, that he does.*
>
> [14] *For he will complete what he appoints for- me, and many such things are in his mind.*
>
> *— (Job 23:11-14, ESV)*

He sees a much bigger picture than I do. He does also have my best interest in mind, even when I'm going through some hard or difficult times. You see, we all face tough times. Even those through the ages, all of us do, Jonah, Peter, Paul, all of us… no one is excluded… it's called life.

What matters is how we *respond* to them. And in *whom* we place our trust during those times.

I will continue to trust the Lord Jesus Christ. Since the accident having lost all that I gained in my life. Being a Pastor, seeing myself on the mission field and working towards it - good health a car and a license, I will be there again, eventually. There's a world out there that needs Him and He wants to use us to tell others, maybe someone as close to us as our neighbors, or someone across the ocean about Him and what He offers. We all have people around us that need help we just may need the persistence to stay with it when times get tough. We need the encouragers when times get difficult. I hope by my sharing this, that it will do just that for you. We are never promised a life free of difficulty. But Jesus says that He will be with us and help us through the difficult times. The Lord sticks closer to us than a brother. That we can count on.

Scripture Share

Behold, I am with you,
and will keep you wherever you go,
and will bring you back to this land.
For I will not leave you until I have done
what I have promised you.

-(Genesis 28:15, ESV)

Encouragement

Stay the course even in the most desolate places of silence... Though we may be now, or have been, asking for something and see no movement, keep hope alive. God is still bigger and in control of everything. He has plans for you and me. There have been times in my life where I feel like God has given up on me. Times when I have been depressed or even angry. We are all human. We are allowed to ask "Why." We just need to remember God is in control. Nothing that happens, no matter how bad it seems isn't known by God, it must pass his desk first and there is always something to be gained from it. A lesson, a slowing down, a test of trust, a molding, a building of faith, a pruning or refining. Whatever God has purposed your pain for, it is for something bigger than ourselves. Believe me, I do believe we are close to the end times, and Christians will be experiencing more trials and tribulations. It's a part of life. Just know that God is in control.

Always in His Will- Mark

JESUS FOREVER CHANGED MY HEART
April May Diaz

My mother was sixteen and my father was forty-two when they got together. You can see from the great age gap that my mom was seduced by her best friend's father. They ended up getting married.

My father was in the Hell's Angels. He was an alcoholic, he was a womanizer, and there was a lot of domestic violence in my home and in my life. I grew up with that kind of violent, angry, influence. So I was *tough*, I mean I had been cussing since I was little.

Thank *God* my mom finally got the courage to leave my father.

She ended up meeting a man named Charlie. He came over one day, because he wanted to meet me and my sister. He said, "I'm going to play some basketball with these girls and get to know them." So we're outside playing basketball and me and my sister don't like the way the games going. I'm eight and she's six.

We start fighting and cussing at each other. We're pulling each other's hair and Charlie's like, "What the heck is wrong with these girls?" He says, "Kathy, they need to go to church." And so my mom agreed, "Okay we'll go to church." So he took us to the First Baptist Church of Bellflower.

That was the first time I ever learned about *Jesus*.

I was liking it. It was nice. Charlie had us all baptized together. Then my mom and Charlie ended up getting married.

So after they were married I remember them sitting us down, that's when they told me that my father had passed away. I got so mad. I was so angry. I was so hurt. I felt this emptiness in my heart. I couldn't explain it. I ran in the bathroom, and I just destroyed the whole bathroom. I ripped the towel rack out of the wall, and I was just acting insane. So Charlie comes in there and says, "Hey, come and sit down. I want to tell you something, "I love you, and I love your sister, and I'm going to adopt you both."

Luckily for me my name is April, and Charlie's last name is May. So yay, I became *April May*. "

When I think back I remember just always filling this empty void ever since my dad died. When we went to church when I was younger, it was fine. My mom was involved. She was involved in Sunday school. She sang in the choir, and it was so cool. But during my teenage years I just didn't like the church. I didn't like the way it was going. I felt like they were hypocrites. There was a lot of gossip, and I was rebelling. I had this void that nobody could fill. I was fighting with my mom. I was fighting at school. I was fighting with males, I was fighting with females. I'm cussing at my teachers, and it was awful.

I started doing drugs and started drinking. I was just trying to, you know, make myself feel better. My mom kicked me out of the house and I ended up getting pregnant, so my mom let me move back in. I had been so out of control! I didn't have my first doctor's appointment until I was in labor. I wasn't taking care of myself at all, so I received no prenatal care that whole entire time.

But thank *God* my son turned out healthy.

And this is what the Lord would use to change my whole entire life.

GOD KNOWS WHAT WE NEED

I stopped doing drugs for good. My son is now thirty-four years old, and I can say with confidence that I know God delivered me from the drugs because I never did them again. In fact… I left my sons father because he *wouldn't* stop doing drugs.

I then ended up meeting my husband who I am married to now, and we have four kids together, so in total I have five kids. ..

ME THEN …

I've always been that kind of tough mom, like, "No one's messing with my kids, that's not gonna happen." I wasn't that gentle kind of mother. You know the kind that gently corrects her children by talking sweetly saying softly, "We don't do that sweetheart." I was more like, "Hey, you know what?... You're gonna get your teeth knocked out., I'm not playing, you're gonna be missing teeth here." And that tough part of me still remained… When I think back it's just like, oh my gosh how awful. I have so many stories about the way I was then, and in contrast you wouldn't even believe I am the same person by the way my spirit has softened now.

> *²⁶ And I will give you a new heart, and a new spirit I will put within you. And I will remove the heart of stone from your flesh and give you a heart of flesh.*
> *-(Ezekiel 36:26, ESV)*

There was a time I worked for my mother in her restaurant and we ended up having a falling out, so I left. She ended up disowning me. She denied me as her daughter and wanted nothing to do with me. She didn't talk to me for three years.

During that time I ended up finding a job at Marie Callender's. Where I met a waiter named Isaac, and all Isaac does is talk about Jesus, and invite people to the church, and his mom would come in to see him.. They're really nice people. They're hugging you. They're inviting you to church. At this point I really try to avoid them because I'm thinking these Jesus freaks are nuts. I didn't want any part of them… They were just overly nice, but I'm like please stop…

Then one day I received news about my mother. She had a stroke and was in the hospital. She couldn't speak or open her eyes.

I decided to go and see her. I walked in the room and wasn't sure if she would know that I was there, or if she would even *want* me there. So I looked at her and said, "Hi mom, its April, do you want me to leave? "She shook her head *no*. That acknowledgement gave me the opportunity I needed, I was finally able to tell her that I loved her. That I was sorry, and that [4]I forgave her. Tears ran down her face. She ended up passing away four days later. I'm glad I got that closure for her and for myself. I thank God that I was able to provide her soul with peace, which in turn gave me peace also. The Lord works even when we aren't aware. Although I hadn't completely surrendered to the Lord. He knew this was something that was so necessary not only for my mother, but for me and my healing...

Colossians 3:12-15 ESV[4] *[12] Put on then, as God's chosen ones, holy and beloved, compassionate hearts, kindness, humility, meekness, and patience, [13] bearing with one another and, if one has a complaint against another, forgiving each other; as the Lord has forgiven you, so you also must forgive. [14] And above all these put-on love, which binds everything together in perfect harmony. [15] And let the peace of Christ rule in your hearts, to which indeed you were called in one body. And be thankful.*

I had no idea what was going to happen, and to my surprise in 2018, my mother would end up leaving her restaurant to me.

KATHY MAYS BY THE LAKE

The restaurant is named after my mother. I, wanting to honor my mother and her memory, refused to sell it. Although it was already in deep debt and made very little money. I wanted to make a go of it so I pressed on. It was *tough*- but so was I. I refused to quit. I made it through a year and by 2019, I found out Marie Callender's was closing. It was then that I brought Isaac over, and I hired him as a server.

Then I watched him again with all the customers, and he had so much joy. And he's so happy. And his mother is always happy. And it's like, why are these people so happy? Well, they kept on praying for me and my salvation. They kept on inviting me to church. They're inviting me to Bible study. But I still don't have any interest of going.

In 2020 Covid happened, and we just about lost everything. We owed so much money that our bank account was in the negative.

Our phones got shut off. I eventually had to use my credit cards to pay the bills and buy food. We could only provide take-out orders. It was just me and my daughter. Some days we wouldn't have any customers. There was no one in the park. I was stressed out and overwhelmed. So I did the only thing I could think to do. I got on my knees and prayed and cried and said "Lord, your will be done" …Although I wasn't attending a church at this time, I put my trust in God completely and He made it happen. We had such a huge line of people that I had to get my cook back. My kids had to come help and my server Isaac. We got super busy! *It was a Miracle*!!! The restaurant belongs to Jesus.

Another miracle happened during Covid, I had been experiencing stomach problems for eight years. Yet all the Doctors I saw would say I was fine. But I *knew* I wasn't. Still it would be God who led me to the right Doctor. Finally I had a diagnosis, it was my gallbladder and it needed to be removed right away. I went to church to receive prayer, and had my surgery. Thank goodness it was successful.

One of the things that I find so important to tell you is to *keep on…* Keep on praying, inviting, and believing that Jesus will make a way. If your reading this and have been praying for someone and inviting them to church and you don't see anything happening just yet. Let me encourage you... never give up! It's so important to keep on extending the olive branch. I am so grateful to the Lord for placing Isaac with me. You see he never gave up... Him and his mother kept on praying and he kept inviting me to his church. [5]He planted the seed ...and God gave the growth.

Finally one day I ended up giving in... I told my daughter, "You know what, let's just go. Let's just go to this church and just see what it's all about and why they're so happy."

So we went to Tuesday night over at Peter's Landing. And when I walked into the church, I was like "Wow," everybody was so inviting, asking if they could pray for us. It was so amazing. I mean, they were all just so welcoming and awesome. So now I'm thinking, "Okay I'm liking this," but I'm still kind of like, these people are weird. But you know what? I kept going. And then I ended up getting even more involved. Our Pastor Joe tells us to

---

[5] *1 Corinthians 3:7 ESV,* [7] *So neither he who plants nor he who waters is anything, but only God who gives the growth.*

say hello to the people around us before we sit down. During that time there was a lady sitting in front of me. She turned around and told me, "You should sign up for the Women's Bible study, the tables right over there." And I was like, "OK, I'm just gonna do it." So I signed up for the Women's Bible Study. And then I started *going* to the Bible study.

I was listening to all these women honestly thinking they're nuts. But I went every day. I listened to them, and God had me be quiet for the first time in my life. Before this, I was always outgoing and constantly talking. And I would always open my mouth when I probably shouldn't. But now here I was… *listening.* I would just listen to these ladies and their beautiful stories, and their inspiration, and their wisdom, and their knowledge. They became like the water that watered the seed. And through my time with them, getting to know Jesus became my singular focus and I started seeing the change in my life. I started experiencing the *growth.*

> *Behold, I am doing a new thing, now it springs forth, do you not perceive it? I will make a way in the wilderness and rivers in the desert.*
>
> -(Isaiah 43:19, ESV)

ME NOW…

I finally stopped cussing. I actually had a real potty mouth. It was really bad. I didn't cuss anymore. I didn't have the desire to do all the bad things that I was doing. I didn't want to listen to Metallica anymore, which has been my favorite band for thirty or forty years. I didn't want to listen to rap. Jesus changed me so much in fact that I didn't even enjoy blaring my music… I used to bump the speaker in my car. But honestly when I really think about it, I mean, I'm fifty and a mother of five. I don't know what was the matter with me. I guess I thought it was so cool. But little by little Jesus changed all that, and now what I really think is cool, is Him. Everything I do is for *Him*. The restaurant belongs to Him. everything I have is His, and I belong to Him also…

Jesus has given me everything…

He gave me a stepfather who took us to church. The birth of my first child to get me off drugs. And then later used an encourager, my server Isaac, who led me back to church, which helped to change my life. The Women's Bible study helped change my life. The women are just an inspiration. I mean, it's all so wild. I ended up surrendering to God completely. I go to Him now for everything. He is like my best friend, and once you make him your best friend its indescribable .. just the peace you have in your soul is amazing.

I have so much more peace and its crazy but every time I walk into church I feel like I'm a part of God's army. It's truly amazing. I now just think 'TRUST IN GOD' and don't fight His will because you can't. And it's really awesome. My son was telling one of my Bible studies sisters. "I don't know what that church is doing to my mom, but I like it." And he started going. He comes Tuesday night with me, so *praise God*. Now if I could only get the other four to come. I also now am just so thankful because I don't just believe in God, I'm walking in God and that's what I've been looking for. That void and that pain that I had all those years, it's just ..it's been filled. I feel joy. I feel peace. I'm a totally different person.

I used to just handle things so differently, like with violence. I had road rage, but I *don't* have that anymore. Somebody cuts me off... I'm just like, "Yeah, go ahead... I love you, have a beautiful day." And then I'll just pray for them.

Only Jesus matters, nothing else. His love for us matters. It's His love that changes our hearts. It can break through even the toughest exterior. This I know because of the way He changed me. His love broke through my toughness and reached down into the pain held in my heart and filled that void. For the rest of my life I just want to glorify Him with everything I do. I want to thank HIM for my church and all the people in it because they're all wonderful, loving, and so kind, and they are all an inspiration… I am grateful to Jesus for saving my life and changing me from the inside out- For the peace, my soul now has, and my softened heart- it is truly a MIRACLE.

Scripture Share

^{16}In the same way, let your light shine before others, that they may see your good deeds and glorify your Father in heaven.

-(Matthew 5:16, ESV)

Encouragement

Let God have complete control. He loves us. We have to trust His plan. Don't fight His will because you can't. Seek Jesus and stay in His word. Make Him your best friend and just watch what He can do. Be the Light!!!

Always in His Presence. April

I HEAR ANGELS
Barbara E. Kompik

It was Christmas time..

The hospital corridor lights were low and the lights on the Christmas tree shone brightly in the foyer.

I left Dale's room at 1:00 in the morning to let his dad stay with him overnight. I gave my husband a kiss good night and walked the length of the hospital to our room, where we had been staying for five weeks straight. People were so kind and so generous to cover the expenses that we incurred for those five weeks. Room and board. Meals at Dale's side. Clothing. Toiletries. Anything we needed, they provided.

Now I was walking alone, wanting to settle in for the night and get my rest for another day with my son. I made my way into the room which was lit with one single light and very still. I paid no attention to it at the time, but got ready for bed and situated myself with a pillow behind my back and the covers up to my chin. I was ready to write again. It was quiet. Just me in our room. A hush fell over the room and I gazed out into the space beyond my bed.

And then I *heard* it…
It was so soft.
It was so faint.
It was so beautiful.

There was *a sound* coming from the space into which I was gazing.

I looked around the room to check to see if any electrical appliances were making this sudden sound. There was no TV. There was no alarm clock. Just this beautiful sound.

I sat there in my bed and listened very intently and very carefully to The Sound that I was hearing. Was I imagining this? I sat and listened more. It sounded like singing. There was a low pitch and a high pitch and a middle pitch to The Sound. And it just hummed steadily for minutes on end. Feeling that I had just heard something very special, I took my pen and paper and began to write. "As I lay my head to sleep, I feel as though I can hear a choir of heavenly Angels ever so faintly away beyond the sky. They are proclaiming Dale's arrival soon. It is a constant stream of high and low sounds mingling together, a never-ending praise and worship of *Jesus in all his glory*."

And then in my mind's eye I saw him. Dale and I were standing side by side on the edge of heaven's golden streets and we were taken by the sight before us, which was angels for as far as we could see, wing to wing, standing before us as in a choir. They were singing and humming. This is the sound that I had heard in the room. And then Dale stepped out from beside me without a glance and without a word, and boldly walked steadfastly towards the choir. He steps up into the ranks of Angel singers and he takes his baritone place within them. Third center to the left. He is home.

"Sing, Dale, sing."

I looked at my watch. It had just struck 2:00 in the morning.

I woke up still thinking of the sound that I had heard in my room those early morning hours. I couldn't shake what my mind's eye had seen and what my ears had heard. But I got up around noon and got ready to go up to see my darling Dale for the day. I made my way up to his room and only his nurse and him were within it. I stepped in quietly. There was a hush in the room and the nurse was moving Dale's equipment very slowly and carefully. "What's going on?" I asked inquisitively. "He's.... going..... I have to move the equipment for room.... I have to call code blue." Do I have time ...? My voice faded into nothingness. Her response was, "Yes. But only about five minutes." I stepped around the bed that my son was laying on, his eyes shut, restful. I gazed at him, knowing it would be my last. I glanced at the machines that read his vitals. The lines were slowly descending. And then she said, "It's time."

I remembered the angels. And I looked at the clock on the wall. The hands were just striking **2:00 p.m**.

AN ENCOURAGING WORD

Though it was the most difficult task I had ever been asked to do, and that was to see my baby boy laying there dying in the hospital bed, my heart cry was continuously, I surrender all. I surrender all. All to Jesus, I surrender. I surrender all…

God had laid on my heart that He was in control, and that my son's life was going to live on in the lives of the people that he had touched and ministered to. And that more lives would be touched through his death. But, oh, how difficult and how gut wrenching it truly was.

A song was shared with me during this time and part of the lyrics say, [6]"The waves and wind still know His name."

- Bethel Music, It is Well.

How could I question a loving and faithful God who knew more than I did regarding my very own son's life?

I surrender all. Yes, I surrender all.

---

[6] "It Is Well" was released in 2015 as the second single from Bethel Music's ninth album, You Make Me Brave. Kristene DiMarco wrote the song, with posthumous credits to Horatio Spafford and Philip Bliss for interpolating the hymn "It Is Well with My Soul"

Scripture Share

*But now thus says the L*ORD,

he who created you, O Jacob,

he who formed you, O Israel:

"Fear not, for I have redeemed you;

I have called you by name, you are mine.

² When you pass through the waters, I will be with you;

and through the rivers, they shall not overwhelm you;

when you walk through fire you shall not be burned,

and the flame shall not consume you.

*³ For I am the L*ORD *your God,*

the Holy One of Israel, your Savior.

I give Egypt as your ransom,

Cush and Seba in exchange for you.

-(Isaiah 43:1-3, ESV)

Encouragement

What I would like to say to a reader who may be going through what I went through…Completely surrender your life, your soul, your circumstance, and your loved ones to the will of the Father, who knows all things before we do. And works everything out for the best possible solution for all of us, even though it doesn't feel like it. We can't trust our feelings. We can only trust God. And that is where our peace comes from.

I surrender all, says it all. All to Jesus, I surrender.

I surrender all. -Barbara E Kompik

THE BOLD PROCLAIMER
Janice Bobanis

My Bazaar Encounter with **_Jesus_**...

Dear Reader, I hope this story accomplishes more than me just talking about myself. I want to inspire and encourage you by sharing my experience as I have traveled this journey with the Lord. As anyone who has been called into ministry knows, the Lord prepares the called. So this is my story...

I grew up in a loving Christian home with two parents and three siblings. We attended church every Sunday and I was active in all the programs a church can offer a young person.

My parents were strong believers. Growing up, I had no reason not to believe everything they had taught me to believe. However, this was my parent's belief. I would soon understand the difference in this kind of belief and actually owning my belief. I have heard that your perception of God is closely related to how you were raised. If you were raised in a home without discipline, then you might perceive God as a winking grandfather type that never disciplines and can overlook sin. If you grew up in a home where the father was very strict and unapproachable, then you might view God as nothing more than a rule maker. However, if you grew up with a father who showed love as well as discipline, then you probably have a healthy and realistic idea of who God is. I was very fortunate in that I had a healthy relationship with my father. He was loving and he was a disciplinarian. I can remember having an active prayer life while I grew up.

When I went to college, I stopped going to church. I *never* read my Bible. In fact, I didn't even take my Bible to college.

I got married right out of college and it wasn't until I was thirty that we had our first child. Two years later, we would have our second child. During this time, someone asked my husband to a Bible study. Over the course of that year, I could see him growing and maturing in his relationship with the Lord. It wasn't long before he recommended I attend the ladies Bible study. I quickly told him that I had a foundation and I didn't need to go. He replied, "But you aren't growing." Well, that cut like a dagger! Long story short, he orchestrated a friend to invite me and so off I went.

There were seven hundred and fifty people in this study. I knew a lot of them but not one person sat by me in the lecture room that first day. I came home and told Jeff I wasn't going back. He told me there was a rhythm to it. If I would agree to give it two months, I could quit if I still didn't want to go. We were in the book of John. Now, here is where it starts to get interesting...

I had recently quit work to stay home with my small children. We were adjusting to one income. The church we attended hosted an annual Christmas bazaar. You could pay one hundred dollars and set up a table to sell your items. Jeff's aunt made these really cute purses and I figured I could get me a table at the church bazaar and make some money! In fact, I had decided how I would spend that money a thousand different ways in my head. I pay my one hundred dollars. I set up my table. Jeff's aunt had said I could keep any profit I made over the cost of her purses. And so, off I went!

I sit at this church bazaar for three days. For THREE DAYS I don't sell a single purse. The lady next to me asked why I hadn't sold any purses. She said, "They are so cute!" I responded, "I know and I am in the hole a hundred dollars!" She quickly quipped back, "But the money goes to the church." I said, "I don't care, I'm in the hole a HUNDRED DOLLARS!" The church bazaar ended and I went home with every one of those stinkin' purses and not a dime in my pocket.

And …did I mention that I was in the hole a hundred dollars?

That Monday morning after the church bazaar, I am doing my lesson. I am almost to the end of my two-month agreement with my husband over this Bible study I had to attend. I get to a question on my lesson. It asked me to look up a verse. It was John 2:16. I can remember exactly where I was sitting and what time of day it was. It was a moment I will *never* forget.

> *To those who sold doves* Jesus *said, "Get these out of here! How dare you turn my Father's house into a market!"*
>
> *-(John 2:16, NIV)*

It was as though the words in my Bible levitated off the page. At that very moment I felt so dirty. In this verse, Jesus was *scolding* the money changers for using the temple for personal financial gain. As a matter of fact, that is exactly what I was doing at the church bazaar. Everything hit me at once. I knew God was intimately involved in my failure to sell a single purse. I knew the timing of that particular Bible study lesson was no accident. God brought me to Jesus at that very moment. I felt so dirty for what I had used the church for. Yet, at the same time, I completely connected the dots as to what Jesus did on the cross. I felt dirty, but then I immediately felt clean because, at that very moment, I got Jesus. My faith instantly shifted from what I was taught to believe to my own belief.

Jesus had met me right where I was.

This was an event in my life that would forever change my trajectory. It was my "born-again" moment. I received the Holy Spirit and my spiritual gift of teaching even though I didn't realize it at that moment.

Sometime later, I was walking through my living room and out of the blue I heard the Lord say to me, "You are special." I don't know if He tells everyone that or if He was letting me know that I had a special purpose He was preparing me for. What I do know is that when I became "born-again" my life took on a new purpose. And so there you have it. That was my bazaar encounter with Jesus!

THE ISAIAH CALL

From that point on, life began to take a new and amazing turn. I continued in this Bible study and later became a children's leader. I wasn't sure that it was the right role for me as I was better with adults than children.

We think we know what is best, but *God* determines our steps.

A children's leader was *exactly* what I needed. God had to prepare me for a future calling and He was doing so even though I was oblivious to it. It's hard to imagine a thirty-five-year-old woman getting nervous in front of preschoolers. However, speaking in front of ANYONE terrified me. God had to start me off with tiny steps. No pun intended! I was trained the basics of teaching scripture to preschoolers. I stayed in this role until my daughter became very sick.

Flu season came. My five-year-old daughter not only caught the flu, but it developed into a serious illness. It was in the quiet nights of the hospital room that the Lord told me my ministry was at home with my family. So, I dropped out of Bible study and gave up my role as children's leader.

Would I have dropped out if my daughter had not gotten sick? I don't know; probably not.

My daughter made a full recovery about two months later. So, I became more involved in my church and in Vacation Bible School. Actually, the church I was attending called it Vacation Church School. This will make more sense in a moment. I attended a meeting for those who wanted to volunteer. During the meeting they asked for a volunteer to direct it. Supernaturally my hand went up in the air and before I knew it, I was the designated Vacation Church School director! I call this my "Isaiah call"!

> *Then I heard the voice of the Lord saying, "Whom shall I send? And who will go for us?" and I said, "Here am I. Send me!"*
> *-(Isaiah 6:8, NIV)*

Yep! Pretty much the Lord was looking for a director and I took Him up on the opportunity!

Being a fairly new "born-again" believer, my passion ran high for the Word of God. After all, the Word of God is what saved me! Remember the verse I told you about that seemed to levitate off the page? It bugged me that this Vacation Church School seemed to be more of a craft fair than teaching the Bible to children. Therefore, I chose to shake things up a bit. I wrote the curriculum myself. I was determined to teach these children the *Word of God* rather than a plethora of craft ideas.

I did this for two summers in a row; writing the curriculum myself. The first year went pretty smooth under the current pastor. The second year was a different story. We had a new pastor and he called me into his office. He made sure I knew I was under qualified to write a Bible study curriculum for children. He made clear, in no uncertain terms, that he was a Bible scholar and I was not.

There was so much passion swirling around inside of me that I knew I must not compromise my convictions. The opportunity to teach God's Word to these children could not be overlooked. So, I pressed forward with my curriculum. The Vacation Bible School was a success! So much so that I received a thank-you note from one of the mothers. She was grateful I had the conviction in my soul to make the necessary changes. And to my knowledge, I believe they kept that vision going.

THE NEIGHBORHOOD AUTHOR

Shortly after that, we left the church as we had moved to a suburb outside the city. We lived in a small neighborhood with four small cul-de-sacs. Because my writing seemed to be a fruitful success, I decided to write a Bible study and invite the neighbors to attend. I invited everyone on the cul-de-sacs. However, I kept hearing the Lord say, "Invite Ellen." Ellen lived around the corner from the neighborhood. But the Lord knew Ellen needed to come! So, I invited Ellen. We started out with one couple and eventually grew to seventeen people. And yes, Ellen came and remained in my Bible studies for the next several years.

Because of my shyness of speaking in front of people, I would write my commentary as notes rather than teaching it orally to the group. For two semesters, I wrote a study. We did the Life of Abraham in the fall and The Book of James in the spring. That following summer, I couldn't come up with what to write for the fall semester.

Always, the Lord clearly laid upon my heart what I was to teach. But it was dead silent. Nothing came to me to write on. The phone began to ring as people were asking when we would start up again. I didn't have an answer for them. I can remember how much I missed the Bible study group. It weighed heavily on my mind every day. One day, I was cleaning the toilet in the girl's bathroom when I remembered this verse...

> *"Whatever you do, work at it with all your heart, as working for the Lord, not for men since you know that you will receive an inheritance from the Lord as a reward."*
>
> *-(Colossians 3:23-24)*

So, I made my mind up that I was going to do that. And boy, were my toilets clean!

THE SPECIFIC CALL

Just a few weeks later, I was ironing and the fact I had not followed through for my neighbors was heavy on my heart. So, I placed the iron in the upright position and headed to my closet where I pray. I mean, where I *really* pray. I had to walk through my bathroom to get to my closet. It was a nice sized closet where I had room to get on my knees. I would face the back of a chair with my hands folded on the seat. It was here that I could block out all the distractions and feel closest to the Lord. I was so frustrated with my situation that I practically spoke out loud in my prayer. In fact, I didn't really ask, I demanded an answer!

I said, "Lord, what do you want me TO DO?" And HE said, "*Janice, your fear of speaking in front of people is in the way of what I have for you.*"

It was not audible. But it was audible. Do you understand what I am saying? I heard the Lord speak to me in a way I had *never* experienced before. I'm still in my closet when I hear the phone ringing. I leave my closet and walk through my bathroom. I see a massive amount of tiny wings in the tub and all over the floor. These tiny wings were not there when I walked *into* the closet. They just appeared as I walked *out*. I did not think they had any significant meaning at the time. I just wanted to know what they were and how they got there. I soon learned they were "termites" and they will have significant meaning later in this story.

I hear the phone ringing so I run to my desk and answer the phone. It is Barbara, she was a friend I had dinner with the night before. I had told her about my frustration with not knowing where to serve the Lord or what to write for my neighborhood Bible study. She was calling me to make a suggestion. She told me she had been thinking about what I had said. She asked me if I had ever heard of another International Bible study that was different from the one I had been a children's leader in. She was wondering if I would consider serving in that Bible study. I had not heard of it. However, I remembered that someone had handed me a pamphlet that was something like she had described. We talked for a bit and then hung up. I remember I had thrown that pamphlet in with a bunch of other papers. It was still there. As I took it out, it had the name of the Bible study she had told me about. Remember, this is all happening within an hour; the prayer, the termites, the phone call, and the pamphlet.

I decide to call the phone number on the back of the pamphlet. I mean, what could it hurt? Maybe this was all connected somehow…I call the number. A lady answers the phone. I begin to tell her about everything that was happening that day. She asked me where I lived. I tell her that I live in Parker County.

AND SHE SAYS, "There's been a group of ladies praying for over a year that God would raise up a leader to start a Bible study class in your county.

My heart dropped at the thought of what *God* was calling me "to do." I *knew* without a doubt He was calling me to teach that class.

This was an international Bible study in which the teacher stands at a podium and teaches to a sanctuary of people. Oh, how scary! She explained that I would have to start a prayer group to raise this class up with leaders and members. So, I called the ladies who had attended the neighborhood Bible study and we prayed every Wednesday for a year and a half over starting this class.

Once we had the leadership in place and sixty people signed up, we could begin the class. During that time, we studied Nehemiah as a small group Bible study/ prayer group. My confirmation verse came to me from the eighth chapter of Nehemiah. Chapter 8 describes Ezra standing above the crowd reading scripture and making it clear, giving it meaning, and making it easy to understand. Once again, it was though the words of those verses levitated off the page! What is amazing about this confirmation is that God gave me the gift of making scripture easy to understand. I have been told this by many of my students.

This proves how intimately involved *God* is in the details of our life.

The following three years and three weeks were some of the most rewarding years of my life. I made so many special friends and saw so many people grow in their knowledge and faith. I was never so terrified in my life as I was the first few weeks I taught. Yet, God grew me and developed my teaching skills. I soon became more comfortable with public speaking. Furthermore, I have never felt so honored and privileged to be called to such a task. This wonderful journey lasted exactly three years and three weeks into the fourth year of our class.

A COURAGE LIKE JOSHUA'S

We had studied several books of the Bible. The fourth year was just beginning and we were studying the book of Joshua. I could feel tension and dissension among three of my leaders. I was told I was being undermined and I could *feel* it. I was not good at confronting others and so I kept hoping it would go away. I can remember the third week of that fourth year, I knew I had a serious problem on my hands.

Unsure of how to handle it, I came home after my lecture, sat in my husband's chair, and prayed that God would make me a strong leader like Joshua.

On the fourth week, I was called into a meeting by my area director. She and three of my leaders told me I was being removed as teaching director. I was *devastated*. I had worked so hard on building this class and preparing lectures. How could God *allow* this to happen? I didn't deserve this. What I now know, is it *had* to happen. God had to teach me the cost of not confronting a problem. I had prayed that God would make me a strong leader like Joshua. He had to show me the cost of not being strong; then He could teach me *how* to be strong.

Remember the termites?..

When I came out of my closet that day, I didn't have a clue they had significant meaning. It wasn't until I had time to reflect that I realized they were a warning. Termites work underneath the surface. They eat away at the foundation of a structure. When you actually see evidence of termites, the damage has been done. This is what the Lord had to teach me. I was naive and timid. I had to learn to call a spade a spade and nip problems in the bud immediately. Weak leadership does *not* glorify God.

> *"Have I not commanded you? Be strong and courageous. Do not be terrified; do not be discouraged, for the Lord your God will be with you wherever you go."*
>
> *-(Joshua 1:9, NIV)*

Shortly after my removal, I had a very brief vision in my head. I saw myself wearing a pair of red sparkly slippers like Dorothy wore in the Wizard of Oz. I was clicking my heals just like Dorothy did so she could return to Kansas. Well, I thought it meant I would return to my Bible study class but that wasn't the case.

A few nights later, I awoke from my sleep and in my head I heard the faint lyrics of a song I loved in my youth. It was titled, Don't You Worry 'Bout a Thing" by Stevie Wonder. I knew the Lord was telling me something but I didn't know what it was exactly. I found comfort in knowing He was letting me know everything would be ok. I took time off to re-evaluate my calling. I continued to do the Bible study lessons the class was doing, though I did it on my own in the quietness of my study. It wasn't until the study got to the book of 1 Samuel 22 that I knew my respite was coming to a close.

I had enjoyed the break. It was a lot of pressure to have a lecture prepared each week while raising a family. But my journey was about to take a new path. Over the yearlong break, many of the women had left the Bible study that I had been removed from. Some were calling and saying if I would start something they would come.

God has a way of making things crystal clear through His word. I was sitting in my study doing my lesson from I Samuel 22. The very first verse I read was:

> "David left Gath and escaped to the cave of Adullam. When his brothers and his father's household heard about it, they went down to him there. All those who were in distress or in debt or discontented gathered around him, and he became their leader. About four hundred men were with him."
>
> -(I Samuel 22:1-2, NIV)

I knew that I was to start a new Bible study class. I began to pray about it. Where would it be? What would I call it? I went into my church office and talked to the staff about it. They were excited for the opportunity and we all agreed that I would start a Bible study class at the church. I was walking in the neighborhood one morning and praying about what I would call it. I heard the Lord say, "wigwaf." I knew I heard it clearly and so I began putting words to the letters and came up with "Women in God's Word and Fellowship." WiGWaF.

For six glorious and blessed years I got to teach those wonderful ladies. It was exactly what I needed. I gained the confidence, the experience, and the knowledge I needed to keep going. I had one brief episode of dissension and boy did I nip that in the bud quick! I had gained the confidence to confront a trouble maker when there is one.

During those six years, I lost my dad and my mother. If you have ever gone through the dying process of a loved one, you can't help but know there is a God. It is as evident in the dying process as it is in the birth of a baby. When my mother was in the hospital a week before she passed, I observed her talking to the ceiling of her room. The nurses said it was normal. Before some people die, they communicate with loved ones in Heaven. One particular day, I approached her room. She was in a deep state of concentration as she was looking up toward the ceiling. I didn't want to disturb her so I waited at the door. When I could see that she had returned her focus to something else, I walked in. She looked straight at me and told me two things she had heard while communicating with Heaven. She told me the Lord spoke to her and said, "Alice, it's time to come home." And then she looked at me and said, "You are going to be a *great evangelist*." Okay. Wow. That was a lot to absorb. She died a week later.

After six years of teaching the Bible study, we were feeling pulled in another direction as far as church membership goes. So, we left the church and I gave up my role as the Bible study teacher. That decade taught me a lot about myself, and about people and how they learn. God used all of my experiences to shape me and make me a strong leader like Joshua. This was to prepare me for the next phase of my calling.

WHISPERS FROM GOD

The next few years would be 'transition years. Our kids were at college, then they graduated from college, and life continued on. I began leading a small group study in my home. The group consisted of about seventeen of my most faithful Bible study ladies. They were my prayer warriors and closest friends. This was a quieter time in my life. I feel as though God designed this time so He could show me deeper things. I can remember hearing "Hollywood." This would pop into my mind at the oddest times. I didn't know what it meant but I remember discussing this with my Bible study ladies. I actually thought I might get to teach a Bible study class my daughter was attending in Los Angeles. I have no idea why this ever entered my mind but I was trying to make sense of what I kept hearing. I still don't know the meaning of what I heard. I do know one thing; if you can reach Hollywood for the Lord, you can influence the world!

I can remember waking one night at 4:11 AM. I woke from a very brief but powerful dream. I was standing on the second floor of a beach house. I stood at a window with wooden shutters opening up to an ocean view. The waves were lipping at the shoreline. There was a light breeze. And suddenly I saw a horse coming towards me across the ocean. Everything about the dream seemed real except the horse. The horse looked like a pencil drawing; a sketch. The horse was running toward me. As it got closer to me, it picked up speed. The horse was white but outlined in pencil. A man was riding it. As I studied what I was seeing, the man on the horse suddenly swooshed past me with great speed. The man on the horse passed me as quick as it had appeared. The dream was over in such a flash I could hardly believe what I had experienced. What could it mean? I began to pray about the meaning. I *knew* it was significant.

Then again, at 4:11 AM a few nights later, I woke up and heard,

"Prepare the way." What did it all mean? I am still not sure.

During this time, I was leading this Bible study in my home. About the fourth year into it, I decided to write a study for the ladies rather than using one from an author. I titled it,

In the Beginning: Genesis 1-11.

It took me eighteen months to write it. I asked the ladies if they would do the study and give me their feedback. They loved it. They said they felt it was informative, life changing, and thought provoking. I was happy with that.

I had dreams of getting it published but wasn't quite sure of how to go about it. My daughter was getting married and wanted me to print up a recipe book with our favorite family recipes for the wedding guests. I called a local publisher. She explained it would be way too expensive. As we were ending our call, I asked if she ever published Bible studies. Ok, this was a God thing. This was exactly what she did. She helped Christian authors get their books formatted and published through KDP Amazon.

In 2021, **In The Beginning: Genesis 1-11** was published under my pen name, *Janice Bobanis*.

No, this is not a joke. I actually prayed about my pen name. My publisher told me to google my real name and see how many people came up. The goal was to be the only one that comes up when googling my name. Well, that didn't happen; many popped up. I began to pray and one night I woke up and heard,.. Janice Bobanis! I went to my phone and googled Janice Bobanis. Guess what? No one popped up! Well, of course that should be my pen name! My earthly father called me that as a child. In fact, he would sing the rhyming song to me every morning as I ate my cereal! As the book ran its course on KDP Amazon, I felt it hadn't reached its full potential. My daughter called WestBow Press and set up a phone interview. She warned me they might not talk to me more than ten minutes or so. They talked to me for an hour and forty minutes. Other than correcting a few thousand grammatical errors, WestBow Press endorsed my book without changing a thing. It was published a second time in 2023 as a revised edition of **In The Beginning: Genesis 1-11.**

BOLD PROCLAIMER

Have you ever taken the spiritual gifts test? Our pastor got our congregation to take it. The results were very interesting but not surprising. At the end of the test, you are given a name. Mine was Bold Proclaimer!

The rest of the story is this…. I don't know what else God has planned for me. I hope and pray that I can continue writing Bible studies. I know from experience that the journey takes sharp curves. The path winds in and out of valleys and mountaintops. Sometimes you can see what is in front of you and sometimes you can't. Sometimes you go through spells where God's voice becomes faint. I have learned that I cannot figure out what God is going to do. His ways are so much better than mine. When things start to come together, I am always amazed at His incredible and powerful orchestration. I believe that some of the visions God gave me are yet to be fulfilled.

I do know one thing is for sure, God does not call the prepared,

[7]He prepares the called. The preparation *is* the journey, my friend! I have become a strong leader like Joshua. I have become a Bold Proclaimer. We shall see if I become a great evangelist!

Serving the purpose for which God created me is the greatest honor of my life. As I rewind the tape since my born-again moment, I can see how every experience was all part of God's plan to groom me into the woman I am today. Blessings to you as you embark on your own journey! Remember, the preparation *is* the journey!

Scripture Share

"And we know that in all things God works for the good of those who love Him, who have been called according to His purpose."

-(Romans 8:28, NIV)

---

[7] *Matthew 9:37-38, NIV-* [37] *Then he said to his disciples, "The harvest is plentiful but the workers are few.* [38] *Ask the Lord of the harvest, therefore, to send out workers into his harvest field."*

Encouragement

I encourage you to be brave. Keep your eyes focused on the mountain top for that is where the Lord wants to take you. You will go through rough terrain on your journey. However, you must overcome the pain to get to the mountain top. God is in total control even though some points on the journey don't make sense to you. Forge ahead because the journey is not over. If you stop when the terrain gets rough, you will miss the opportunity to see your purpose fulfilled.

Stay strong and have a blessed journey, my friend!

Janice Bobanis

A CHRIST FOLLOWERS LIFE
Hans Jacob

PHILLIPINES

I consider myself just a normal person like anybody else. Living like a normal kid, getting dirty, spanked by my parents, and growing up. My parents being religious always took us to a big church. But here comes a moment of my life that I feel missing…

I remember feeling *thirsty for something spiritual.*

At a very young age, I feel empty in the spiritual part of me. Though we were attending church every Sunday, someone knocked on our door and introduced Jesus to us. We don't know why, but normally if someone brings a Bible and knocks on our doors, we immediately say "NO." But during that visit, we allow this person to come in into our small house. This person is a crippled man. He brought a plastic of newly baked bread with him and a Bible. He shares Jesus with us. We just found out that he is a pastor. On that day we receive Jesus as our Lord and Savior. We attended to the church where he is doing his ministry. We are moved with every song that we hear, until such time that we don't even notice that we are now part of the ministry. We we're involved in the ministry since then.

Then I meet my wife when I was nineteen years old. The relationship was hard since she is not a believer, but by the grace of God she was able to accept Jesus Christ as her Lord and Savior. We we're blessed with four beautiful and healthy children, and as a father I need to work to provide the basic need for my family. I worked overseas. I worked in SAUDI ARABIA for four- years.

On my first month, a colleague invited me to a birthday party. But as soon as we arrive to the place, it was a church service. I never thought that there is Christian churches inside a Muslim country like Saudi Arabia. This was amazing to me as my soul longs to worship the Lord even when I'm away from my home country. The church is my home and family in Saudi Arabia. Time passed by the calling of the Lord for ministry did not stop in my home country. The Lord still calls me for ministry even into this place.

I was being ordained as Deacon to Elder and an Evangelist. Being an evangelist inside the Muslim cultured country is very challenging. Starting from an underground Church to sharing the Word of God privately. If you get caught sharing Jesus, you will be in trouble.

But the fire of the Holy Spirit in sharing the love of *Jesus* is more *powerful* than fear.

We went to stores, malls, markets, waiting sheds, beaches, parking lots, anywhere we are as long as we have the chance to share the Salvation from the Lord we will. Glory be unto God, because of the work of the Holy Spirit the churches inside the country was growing in numbers. A Christ followers' life is never easy. We are called to serve the Lord and to serve other people by sharing the good news…

THE GREAT COMMISSION

16 Now the eleven disciples went to Galilee, to the mountain to which Jesus had directed them. 17 And when they saw him they worshiped him, but some doubted. 18 And Jesus came and said to them, "All authority in heaven and on earth has been given to me. 19 Go therefore and make disciples of all nations, baptizing them in[a] the name of the Father and of the Son and of the Holy Spirit, 20 teaching them to observe all that I have commanded you. And behold, I am with you always, to the end of the age."

- (Matthew 28:16–20, ESV)

As a follower of Christ, I always put my trust in God. As we live a normal life, facing trials, troubles, difficulties, and circumstances. Falling short by committing bad decisions. We must never lose hope and faith in Lord. [8] (John 16:33). But let us

---

[8] John 16:33, ESV-*33 I have said these things to you, that in me you may have peace. In the world you will have tribulation. But take heart; I have overcome the world."*

not also forget that we are on the last days. The enemy is doing double time to pull us back to him. That's why in our daily lives we must seek the Lord first to be guided and finding a way to get away from temptations…

> *³ No temptation has overtaken you that is not common to man. God is faithful, and he will not let you be tempted beyond your ability, but with the temptation he will also provide the way of escape, that you may be able to endure it.*
>
> *-(1 Corinthians 10:13, ESV)*

Scripture share

> *Blessed is the man who remains steadfast under trial, for when he has stood the test he will receive the crown of life, which God has promised to those who love him*
>
> *- (James 1:12)*

Encouragement

Look into the promises of God. Take hold of them. They will keep you going and find strength and purpose in life. Whatever may block your way, think of God. He is bigger than your worries, temptations, circumstances, and trials. *God loves you* and never leaves you.

My question will *you* respond to His love?

Hans Jacob

✝

ALWAYS WITH THE LOVE OF JESUS
Didier Kwizera

RWANDA

My name is Didier Kwizera, I'm married to Lilian, and God blessed us with two girls (Ynna and Ysalis). I was born and grown in a Christian family. My dad is a pastor in the Anglican church, my mom helps him in a ministry. You can imagine how the pastor's kids are always pushed to be and walk in presence of God.

In my country (Rwanda) we had a tragedy that divided Rwandans into two parts that hated each other. It started in 1959 when some people including my grandfather were hunted to be killed by one group of people. When my grandfather saw what is happening, he fled and went to Burundi and became a refugee there with his family (my father was seven years old at that time).

My father grew up and got married there. I was born there as the fourth child in the family in a very hard situation. I remember that we lived in hut at that time. It was not easy for my dad to provide everything we needed, because we were refugees and didn't have enough to satisfy our needs. We came back to our country in August 1994 right after the Genocide against the Tutsi (I don't want to say much about this genocide, it was such a terrible thing)

When we got back to Rwanda, I was raised in church, every Sunday I used to attend Sunday school, so going to church became a routine to me. My dad used to tell us that God is the source of everything. But I used to complain asking God why we suffer? You can imagine how hard it was for my father to provide for a family of more than ten people (we were seven children and dad used to bring different children to our home regularly).

In 2002, I went to a boarding school and here is when I started to be myself. From that time of early teens, I stopped attending Sunday services and other Christian activities, and joined a group of non-believers. I became immoral and did what my heart desired. But in the holidays, I used to lie to my parents so that they would believe I was a good Christian. Remember, my dad is a pastor and he prayed for me and my siblings every time for God's protection a guidance to our lives. When I finished O' Level (3 years of high school), I changed schools. *My* plan was to get there and become a great basketball player, enjoy my life, and find a beautiful girl to be in love with (I can laugh at myself whenever I remember this).

I didn't expect that I would find someone who knew me in my new school. Then in my first week there, I met with brother in Christ Justin who lived in our neighborhood, and I was surprised with that. He suddenly invited me in the fellowship because he knew my dad as a servant of God.

I remember that day when I was in the service and the preacher shared the Good News of Jesus, saying that He is able to carry my burden of sin. At that time, the Holy Spirit convinced my heart to receive Jesus as my Savior. That was in 2006. I remember I cried and stood up to receive and embrace His forgiveness. From that time on, I start to follow *Jesus*.

From that day my life began to change, and the *Holy Spirit* began to teach me more about God using His Word.

In 2010, I went to university in a *miraculous way*. Actually, I didn't have good enough results from high school for me to get government scholarship. So I took the time to pray- asking God where He wanted me to go? Miraculously, God answered, He put a person in my life who told me that they were going to pay for my university. When I got there, Jesus connected me with a group of His people. These people helped me to grow spiritually because they taught me how to read the Bible on a daily basis, and then, that's where the Spirit of God started to develop a preaching gift in me.

When I began to preach in my church, people and church elders told me that I could start thinking about being a pastor, but I didn't like that. My dad is a pastor in the Anglican church of Rwanda as I said before. I knew the pastoral hardships and challenges. I wanted to be a good IT person and earn good money to provide for my family's need, but people continued to encourage to pray about being a pastor and shepherd God's people. I resisted that so much. After my graduation with Distinction, I tried my best to find a good IT job, but I failed and spent three years without job. I can confidently say that it was God who closed that door allowing Him to guide me into the right way.

> *⁷ "And to the angel of the church in Philadelphia write:The words of the holy one, the true one, who has the key of David, who opens and no one will shut, who shuts and no one opens.*
> *-(Revelation 3:7, ESV)*

In 2018, I was called by one of the bishops of our church and asked me to work together with him in ministry. He wanted me to be in charge of youth and children's discipleship ministry. I got an experience from there, and after one and five months, I moved to the other office. In February 2020, I was appointed to lead mission and training in what we call Kigali Diocese. God was trying to convince my heart to enter into pastoral ministry. It finally happened in the beginning of 2023 I knelt down before God asking *Him* to show me what *He* wants me to do? The Bishop then asked me if he can appoint me to lead local church somewhere.

After praying with my sweet wife, God convinced us to enter into pastoral ministry.

I praise God for that.

I was appointed to the small local church located in the village on the top of the mountain. It is Twelve- miles from my house, and it is in community of poor, drunkard, and adulterous people. They really need Jesus, and I praise God for choosing me to be His vessel used for His glory in these people.

I'm looking forward to see how *Jesus* will transform these people. To conclude, I want to encourage parents to pray for their children and be always present for them. I can assure you that when you pray asking God's guidance, He will use different ways to guide you where *He* wants you to be. And those who don't see the way of how God can use them, I can tell them to fix their eyes only to Jesus, who knows where they can fit in His ministry.

Scripture share

Therefore, since we are surrounded by such a great cloud of witnesses, let us throw off everything that hinders and the sin that so easily entangles. And let us run with perseverance the race marked out for us, ² fixing our eyes on Jesus, the pioneer and perfecter of faith. For the joy set before him he endured the cross, scorning its shame, and sat down at the right hand of the throne of God. ³ Consider him who endured such opposition from sinners, so that you will not grow weary and lose heart.

-(Hebrews 12:1-3, NIV)

Encouragement

I would like to encourage you to keep trusting in the Lord. He is the one who has the plan for your life. Unless you keep your eyes focused on Him, your life will be messed up and you will get disappointed. I am living proof of what Jesus can do in your life.

Saved by Grace to serve God ~

Didier

✝

THE GOOD LORD WATCHING OVER
Carl and Kay Redlin

This event happened over twenty- years ago...

My wife and myself were business owners in Utah and because we advertised on TV channels, we had won a trip to China. So we were going to China with about a dozen other people doing the same thing.

We had left Salt Lake City one early morning. And we had to refuel in Alaska. I don't remember what airline it was, but we had to refuel in Alaska and that meant we had to get off the airplane. While we were sitting there in the lobby, a guy came up to us and said, "We can get you to China 2-3 hours earlier than you're scheduled to get there now. The airplane is going to be leaving here very soon if you would like to get on that flight." However we chose to fly out on the second flight.

So we took off in about 2:00 in the morning. Here we are trying to sleep when the chap in the seat in front of me turns around and wakes me up saying that they lost contact of this airplane in front of us. Well, being a pilot, I thought that that stuff does happen, so we went back to sleep.

After we landed there was a big commotion in the lobby. And we were informed that that airplane that *we could have been on* was in fact shot down by the Russians. This was during the Cold War.

It's still hard to believe that we could have been on that plane that was shot down. We were lucky. My wife Kay when we were trying to decide to go on that flight, looked at me and said, "No, let's stay with the people we met over here and go on our usual planned flight with our new friends." and that's what happened.

The people who were on that first flight were killed instantly.

We found out later that the airplane had drifted into Russian territory. That started it all, there were a lot of other things happening in the world during that time, but that was the one we were almost got caught in. That was one close call. The good Lord was definitely watching over us.

We have gone on to enjoy many more years together, having the most wonderful lives. Kay and I both agree that was one of the more interesting parts..

It was very unusual…

Who would ever think that a Commercial flight would be shot down by a Russian aircraft? It just didn't make any sense. We are grateful that *The Good Lord* stepped in. Today I am still enjoying my life with my beautiful wife Kay. We are still going strong enjoying our time together. We are truly blessed.

Scripture Share

The LORD is my shepherd; I shall not want.
² He makes me lie down in green pastures.
He leads me beside still waters.
³ He restores my soul.
He leads me in paths of righteousness
for his name's sake.
-(Psalm 23:2-3, ESV)

Kays Encouragement

Life is profoundly beautiful, it's not always easy, but it's worth it. Time flies so quickly we must remember to enjoy it all, and count our blessings.

Keep it moving, God Bless-

Carl and Kay Redlin

✝

ROSE, HIS GOOD LESSON
Bonnie McBride

When I first became a Christian, I thought I would be able to tell *anyone* about the Lord...

I would evangelize for Him and witness for Him, everywhere I went and to everyone I would meet. I was on fire with love for Him and with gratitude for what Jesus has done for me. My salvation was a huge gift. I had wanted the assurance of my salvation all my life and now I had it, and I was overjoyed. But I found that many or most of the people I knew didn't want to hear what I had to say. They didn't believe God would speak to you, that salvation was a free gift, or that there was only one way to receive salvation, through Christ's death on the cross.

So, I became a little gun shy. Seeking only the people I was willing to be silly with, people I loved as much as myself.

It was easier to witness to people I liked and loved than to those I didn't really care about. God made me aware of this in a very personal way.

It was the second Christmas after I became a Christian. I was trying to teach the kids the true meaning of Christmas and we were baking cookies and making candy to share with some of our neighbors. Maureen and Kevin came running into the house to tell me that an ambulance had pulled up to a house down the street. They had watched while the attendants had unloaded a passenger and she was taken into her home on a gurney. We didn't know these particular neighbors' and we were concerned that something was terribly wrong.

Immediately the kids wanted to take her a plate of cookies and fudge. Off they went to deliver the goodies, and when they came home they were really delighted at having given the gifts to everyone. It was a great day to be alive and we all felt wonderful about what we had done.

The following day, there was a knock at the door. I was amazed to find a woman standing there in her nightgown, hugging the plate of cookies, and thanking us for giving them to her. She was the woman who had just come home from the hospital the day before and no one had ever done anything like that for her since she had been in our neighborhood. We invited her in, and she began to tell us a little about herself. Her name was Rose, and she was from Korea. She was very sick but was feeling a little better and she wanted to come to thank us and find out who we were. Her English was very broken with a strong accent, and I could only understand a few words.

This was a very uncomfortable situation for me, it was very intense, unfamiliar, and I didn't really know what to say to someone who was so sick- hard to understand and very different than me. My husband had been stationed in Japan during his army years and was more capable of understanding what she said. Rose seemed to feel that because we had sent a gift to her, she was now involved in our lives. She asked what our plans were for Christmas, and we told her we were going to open presents early and then go to Christmas mass before joining the family for dinner.

We didn't extend any invitations, but Rose told us she would go to church with us and asked, "What time should she be ready"? She left the house, and we were left scratching our heads, bewildered at what had just happened.

Later, on Christmas Eve, my husband and I were assembling Christmas toys and getting everything set out for the next morning when we had another visitor. This time it was Rose's husband, and he had come to introduce himself and say hello. I don't recall his name after so many years, only that he was from Japan. He told us a little about Rose's illness. As I remember, it was caused by the water in Korea. Both Rose and her brother suffered from a form of cirrhosis of the liver, and her brother had already died. And this was what was happening to Rose's liver, it was failing. Pat and I listened, and I tried to understand, all the while wishing he would leave because we had things to do, and time was running out.

Christmas morning began with a bang; laughter, excitement, giggles, urging us to get up even though we only had a couple hours of sleep. By the time presents were opened, we ate some breakfast and the seven of us were getting ready for church but we we're running late.

As we were dressing, the doorbell rang, and there was Rose, dressed up and ready for church. By the time we arrived, mass was over, the doors were locked! Rose seemed so disappointed that it was over, so we decided to drive to another parish to see if they had a later service and maybe we could attend.

We arrived at Saint Angela's just as mass was finishing. We sat in the back and stayed until most of the people left the church. By then the Spirit of God was beginning to breakthrough our selfishness and placed upon my husband's heart that Rose needed prayer.

She didn't know who Jesus was, she wasn't a Christian, but she knew God was her only hope and she wanted Him to help her. So, Pat prayed for her healing, for her comfort and well-being, and thanked the Lord for putting her in our paths. We took Rose home and went on our merry way.

A week or so later, Rose invited us to come to dinner at her home, and she wouldn't accept no for an answer. We were overwhelmed by her persistence and couldn't get out of the invitation. The kids were wondering what we would eat, what they would do, how we would all communicate because of their strong accents and our inability to understand. We did a lot of shaking our heads, trying to look interested, and hoping the time would go by fast.

There were lots of different smells in their home, as well as different styles of furnishings. You could smell kimchi the moment you opened the door. And Rose and her husband were cooking dinner. They had two grown sons, who were also there. They didn't seem very pleased to have us over and left as soon as they could. Pat handled the situation far better than I did. I felt as if I was in a play. Acting interested when I wasn't, acting as if I understood when I didn't. Acting as if I was enjoying myself when I wasn't. I was being totally condescending, for Rose's sake, to be an example to my children and to serve Jesus.

Even though I wanted to be elsewhere, there was a burden in my heart to share the salvation message with Rose, but I didn't know how. I was groaning and moaning the whole time. Finally dinner was over, and we all left relieved and glad that it was finished. Now, she paid us back and we could go on with our lives.

But **God** had other plans.

I was led to try to figure a way to share the gospel with her. At that time, Christian television was highlighting the ministry of Nora Lam. She was organizing crusades and ministries to Korea, and I thought I had found a solution to my problem. I called the studio trying to see if I could reach someone who might be able to supply me with a Korean Bible so I could give this to Rose. I tried a couple of halfhearted calls over the next week or so but was unable to get a Bible sent to me for whatever reason.

The following weekend, we were going to the Sportsman Show and were getting ready to leave, when Rose showed up on our porch to visit. We were surprised to see her but when we explained we would be leaving shortly; we were more surprised to hear her say, "*I go with you!*" This was something we weren't used to, someone including themselves in our plans, not asking to come along, not waiting to be invited, but just including themselves. We knew we would be doing a lot of walking, and it was evident that Rose couldn't walk that far or be on her feet that long. Pat and I and the kids were concerned for her well-being, but also feeling Rose would interfere with our fun. Nevertheless, Rose went with us.

It was indeed a very difficult time. We had to sit for long periods, while one of us showed the kids around and one of us took turns sitting with Rose. I found myself resenting her presence, groaning inside that God kept putting her in my path, and I didn't like it. It was hard to be a Christian and show Christian love to someone who was so difficult and so different.

I didn't see Rose for a couple of weeks, but I was telling everyone I knew about this weird woman, wondering how I was going to explain the gospel to her because I felt so inadequate. At that time, I was a member of Woman's Aglow and it was time for our monthly meeting. One of my kids got sick and I wasn't able to attend. But my friend Katrina did. Katrina was the one I shared with the most regarding my feelings about Rose.

We laughed over the strange events and wondered what in the world God had in mind.

Katrina arrived at my house after the meeting and was so excited. Every meeting I attended at Woman's Aglow had a male spiritual advisor in attendance. They were normally Pastors' known to the leadership and invited by them. On this particular day, the Pastor was a visitor from a church in Korea. He was introduced to the women and opened the meeting with a prayer.

After the meeting, Katrina asked to speak with him, and explained my situation and asked how I could witness to Rose. The Pastor took his old worn Bible out of his shirt pocket and wrote the salvation message in Korean on the front page. He gave his Bible to Katrina without a moment's hesitation. And now, Katrina was giving it to me for Rose!

I was overwhelmed by God's provision and timing. But, if I gave another gift to Rose it would start the whole series of "you do something for me," "I do something for you" all over again. I was reluctant to take it to her. A couple of days later, I saw Rose in front of her house, not looking very well. I didn't want to stop, because I was headed to school to pick up my kids, but I yelled to her that I had something for her and hurried off to school. I believe it was two days later that there was a knock on the door. I opened it to find Rose standing there, dressed in a nightgown, telling me that she wanted what I had for her right now! I was taken aback and grabbed the Bible and gave it to her. I remember seeing her clutch it to her chest as she was headed home.

That was the last time I saw Rose. She died three days later.

I was broken hearted! Ashamed of my selfishness! I was remorseful for all my stupid feelings of being uncomfortable, and feeling inadequate. I was, but God wasn't. I had made it all about me. God wanted Rose to be saved and He chose a foolish, self-centered person to be involved in the process. He showed me that even though I was reluctant, He wasn't.

Jesus saved her in spite of me. Thank God!

He taught me that it *isn't* all about *me* and what *I* can do. It is all about *Him* and what *He* can do. All I have to do is say *yes*. He showed me how selfish I was regarding whom I wanted saved, and for whom I would put myself out for. And it was for all the unpleasant, difficult, different people that I didn't care about, but He did.

I praise *God* for this lesson.

He showed me He will make things happen regardless of my cooperation. I could participate and watch Him and be His partner, or I could kick and scream and be a reluctant pawn. The choice was mine; the glory was His. He showed me who I am when I rely upon myself, instead of relying upon Him.

What a Glorious God He is, ...

to be faithful to Rose's prayer, "I *want* what you have for me!"

Scripture Share

He has told you, O man, what is good; and what does the LORD require of you but to do justice, and to love kindness, and to walk humbly with your God?

-(Micah 6:8, ESV)

Encouragement

Whenever I think about the story of Rose, even fifty years later, I am awed by God's love and patience. I was a new Christian and just beginning to experience God being real and moving in my life. I had no idea how to witness to others but I knew Jesus loved me, and died for me and forgave me and set me free. What I learned was that He has a plan for all of us and can accomplish it with or without our help. All He asked of me was to be willing and obedient and He would do the rest.

It didn't matter if I had all the answers, knew the "right" things to say or even liked what I was doing. He would use me in spite of myself and all my failures and I have been so grateful. I don't want to miss out on what He is doing in my life or others. One thing for sure is that He gets the glory!

I cried when I heard Rose died, and felt such shame at my attitude of impatience, and my failures. But Jesus assured me He had my back, He could finish the job and all I had to do was show up and let Him. He saved Rose both on the cross and at my front door!

What does the Lord require of *you*, but to do justice, to love kindness and to walk humbly with your God.

In Spite of Myself, Bonnie

✝

IT ONLY TOOK FIFTEEN YEARS
Candy J. Beard

We've all heard the phrase,

"Everything happens in God's time, not our own."
And my story is a perfect example of just that.

I can remember the first time my family and I visited North Carolina. I remember it as if it just happened last month. When that trip was planned, the year was 2007 and my husband and I were going to be celebrating our twentieth wedding anniversary on April 02, 2008. My husband Mark asked me, *"How would you like to rent a beautiful beach house in North Carolina for an entire week for our anniversary?"*

I said, *"Tell me more"* so he took me to the computer and sat me down and he had already been researching a town called Top Sail Island and had found a handful of absolutely astonishing million-dollar homes that would allow middle class people like us to stay in the homes while on vacation.

I asked him, *"Can we afford this?"* and he told me that we could because they would let us pay a deposit and then make monthly payments until it was time to go the following April. He then asked me if we should take our boys with us, despite it being our twentieth anniversary. We've always been the kind of parents who have wanted to include our two sons in everything.

You see, Mark and I both grew up very, very poor, wearing hand-me-downs, getting free school lunches and free books and sadly, being teased for being poor. And, on top of that, neither of us could ever remember going on a family vacation during our childhood years. So we wanted to give our boys a much better and memorable life than either of us ever had.

So it was no surprise to me that he would ask if we could take our sons on our anniversary trip, and it was no surprise to Mark when I replied, *"Yes, let's absolutely take the boys on vacation with us!"* And, additionally, we had two nephews that were the same ages as our boys. Bobby and Matthew were my sister's sons. Matthew was born just two months before Daniel in 1989 (making the boys eighteen years old at this time) of making plans for April 2008. And her youngest son, Bobby, was born five months before our son Christopher (making them both sixteen years old) at the time we were making plans.

I mention their ages because due to them being so close in age, these four boys were raised more like brothers than just cousins. Bobby and Matthew found our home to be much calmer, more loving and much more fun than my sister's home, so it was no surprise from a very early age, they adopted the habit of wanting to spend summers and every school holiday off with us. And this went on for many years. And while most people would think Mark and I were crazy to say we were taking four teenage boys with us on our twentieth wedding anniversary getaway; to us, it just made perfect sense.

Bobby and Matthew, just like us, had never been on a vacation to a beach before, because my sister hated traveling (and beaches) and did not vacation, so this was an incredible treat for my nephews and Mark and I were excited and proud that we could offer our favorite nephews this amazing opportunity.

Before we could book and make it official, I had to call my sister up and ask her if she would allow us to take the boys. She said she thought we were absolutely out of our minds to take four teenage boys on an anniversary trip, but said, *"More power to ya --- with one condition."* That condition was that we had to go the third week of March instead of the first week of April (anniversary week) because that was when her boys were on spring break and she would not let them miss any school. Our sons were home schooled and since we really wanted her boys to be able to go, we agreed to go in March instead of April. We were, after all, the coolest and favorite Aunt and Uncle in the family. Lol.

So, that day in 2007, we made the commitment and we paid the down payment on a marvelous four bedroom, three story beach home in Top Sail Island, North Carolina. We were so excited, but because it was ten months away, I had to be careful and tiptoe around my sister so that she would not change her mind and revoke the permission she had given me to take her sons with us. She has a temper and usually lives by the motto, "My way or the highway."

But before we knew it, it was March 2008. And by this time, my husband had asked if we could drive through Mount Airy, NC and stop for the night before heading on to Top Sail Island to the beach house. Anyone who is a fan of the Andy Griffith Show knows that Mount Airy, NC is the birthplace to actor Andy Griffith. We were able to rent the actual house that Andy grew up in. It had been purchased by a major hotel chain and used as an Airbnb, just five months before Airbnb was actually established nationwide.

It was a blast for us to stay in Andy's home. The home was so charming and had memorabilia from the show all around it. While in Mount Airy, we took a tour around town in a patrol car. We visited the museum and also stopped at Wally's filling station, the Jailhouse/Courthouse and ate dinner at Goober's Restaurant and finished the day by visiting the drugstore to get sundaes and milkshakes (aka old-fashioned sodas). The next morning we got up and went to breakfast at Barney's Restaurant and then walked through the shops downtown and bought souvenirs and such. We had an extraordinary time. And when it was all done, it was time to load back into the SUV and drive the additional four hours to our beach home vacation rental where we anticipated having the time of our lives.

The beach home was absolutely everything we hoped it would be. It was breathtaking! On a daily basis, we watched the dolphins from the breakfast table. Since it was March, the beach was just the way I like it: very quiet and secluded. It was the first real vacation any of us had ever had and it was amazing. My husband said to me one day while walking the beach and picking up seashells ... *"I could really get used to this, couldn't you?"* and I replied, *"Oh yeah."* And then he said, *"I'm really serious. Would you like to live near the beach one day? Maybe when I retire we could move to North Carolina. Would you like that?"* and I again replied, *"Oh yeah."* And then he followed that up with, *"There would be no more brutal Indiana winters."* And I replied, *"That would be great."*

For anyone reading this who has never experienced Indiana in the winter – oh boy, thank your lucky stars. And thank the good Lord. Mark and I both grew up in Indiana and the older we got; the more we hated Indiana winters. Indiana residents can expect subzero temperatures in the winter with lots of snow and ice. And to briefly walk the beach and think about leaving those harsh winters behind definitely put smiles on our Hoosier faces.

On March 20, 2008, our nephew Bobby turned seventeen and of course we celebrated by taking him out to eat at the restaurant of his choosing (Seafood was his desire) and I bought a birthday cake and ice cream and we celebrated there at the beach house. Bobby said that was the best, most special birthday he ever had. The boys spent their days on the beach but spent their evenings playing video games. It was an incredible week for all four of them and Mark and I enjoyed seeing the joy on their faces. So in a sense, it was like it was everyone's anniversary. The week went fast and before we knew it, our vacation was over and on the way home, we promised that we would definitely return to North Carolina.

That March 2008 vacation would be the only time we ever rented a big, million-dollar beach home to vacation in. It would be the only time we traveled with four teenage boys, and it would mark our only stay in Topsail Island. However, in August of 2013, Mark and I would take another trip to North Carolina. This time, however, Daniel was twenty-three years old and had no desire at this point in his life to go with us. However, Christopher was all for going back to Mount Airy, despite having trouble with nine-hour car rides due to some serious knee injuries. So now there were just three of us.

We did all the same things in Mount Airy in 2013 that we did in 2008, with the exception that this time we stayed in a hotel because the Andy Griffith home was already occupied. And this trip, Christopher was able to get a haircut at Floyd's Barbershop by none other than the actual barber who cut Andy Griffith's hair as a boy. He thought that was pretty awesome.

This trip, however, we stopped to see an actor friend of ours in Charleston, SC (Richard Bryant of *ARMY WIVES*) and visited their beach instead of stopping at a beach in North Carolina. But it was still a great vacation and again caused Mark to mention one day making North Carolina our permanent home. In his mind, he would have to wait until he retired. He was forty-nine years old and figuring he would try to retire at sixty-two, he said, *"I know it still seems like a long way off… thirteen more years, but it's nice to dream about, isn't it?"* and I replied, *"Sure is."* I suppose if I am really being honest and sincere, I think I thought, *"This is a pipe dream, but I can't rain on his parade."*

Ever since the day I met him in nineteen eighty-seven, he had always been an incredibly hard-working man. In fact, I always told people that next to my own father, I had never known a man who worked harder than my Mark. He was actually a work-a-holic and I was tremendously proud of his work ethic. By this time, we had been married for twenty-five years and he had always provided for our family, never being without work. So, if it made him happy to believe that his wife shared his dream of one day moving to a much warmer climate and living near the ocean, I wanted to bring him that joy. Oh I wanted that too. But did I really believe it was possible? After all, we were just a middle-class couple and I guess I suspected it was a dream that was out of our reach, financially because moving nine hours away would be very costly. But then again, God already knows our heart's desires.

Here's a little side note about my husband. I had already mentioned that we both grew up really poor. And when I say poor, I mean food stamps poor. But my husband had to get his first job at age twelve. His father started a trash pick-up business and he made Mark go work for him. While it completely broke my heart to hear this story for the first time (early on in our marriage), Mark says that even though he absolutely hated it when he was a kid and his classmates teased and bullied him for it, he says that it is what built his work ethic to be what it still is today at age sixty.

I never met my father-in-law because he died six years before I married Mark. But if I could have met him, I would thank him for putting his youngest son to work (not alongside his three older brothers either) but just little, scrawny Mark, who if he had been born a cat would have been the runt of the liter. Because this made Mark the man he is today and for that, I am one grateful wife.

Okay, so now I jump ahead to 2017 and once again, my wonderful husband decided to make our anniversary plans. (I just don't have the patience to do this.) He surprised me with our very first cruise to the Bahamas. We had an incredible time and because we are very low-key homebodies, we spent the majority of our time on the very top deck, where it was extremely secluded. Most times, there would only be about three to five couples on the entire top deck and we couldn't have loved that more. We talked a lot as we sat quietly on the lounges soaking up the sun. We talked about how much we missed our sons back home and we talked again about how one day we hoped to live in North Carolina when Mark retired. We talked about warm climates verses brutal winters. And we ate a lot of great food too, ha-ha.

Because the following year would mark our thirtieth wedding anniversary Mark wanted to once again take me back to North Carolina. So in January of 2018, he did all the research himself and was convinced that I would love Atlantic Beach. It's a small beach town with a population of less than fifteen thousand. He found a cute little Airbnb literally right on the beach. He asked that I approve the place and when I did, he booked it. He also booked our flights. Now, all we had to do was count down the days until we left on March 31st. We flew into the Jacksonville, NC airport and unfortunately, the airline lost my luggage.... not our luggage, just Candy's luggage. I was so bummed and frustrated.

The woman who owned the home we rented (the Airbnb) had specifically asked us to call her upon arrival to let her know we made it in okay and to see if we needed anything additional. So upon arrival I phoned her and during our conversation, I mentioned how the airport lost my luggage. She asked, *"What size are you?"* And I was like, *"Excuse me?"* She asked again, *"What size do you wear? I would like to bring you some clothes."* You could have knocked me over with a feather. I could not believe this total stranger wanted to bring me clothes. I mean, I could have just as easily gone to a local store and purchased clothes. But she insisted on blessing me. I told her my clothing sizes and mentioned I wanted to lie down and take a nap, for I had not slept well the night before and had to be at the airport so bright and early that morning. So she said, *"Yeah, you guys go ahead and take a nap. I'll just bring some things over and leave them at the front door for you."* And she did! This angel in disguise actually went out and bought me the cutest clothes, including underwear. I could not believe it. My only regret was that I did not get to meet her in person.

Mark and I had the best time in Atlantic Beach. The people were so friendly, the restaurants were delicious and the city of Atlantic Beach was just awesome. And, bonus: there were not too many people on the beach the first week of April, so again, it felt like we had our own private island and it was incredible. We walked the beach daily, looking for konka shells. We even took back a small jar of beautiful white sand with us. Our last evening on the beach was bittersweet. We took several photos. We got misty eyed that night knowing we had to leave very early the following morning. We had to get up at 6:00 AM to get to Jacksonville to catch our flight back to Indiana. I remember not sleeping very well that night. But we woke up the following morning and put our belongings in the car and then he asked me did I want to take a quick walk back down to basically say goodbye. So we did.

He doesn't want to admit it, to this day, but we both shed some tears that morning. We made a pact with each other that morning in April, two thousand and eighteen and that pact was this ... *We were now putting a move to North Carolina into our five-year plan.* And unlike five years earlier when I wanted it too but didn't really think it was possible (yee of little faith) on that particular day, I really did believe it. In fact, I believed it so much that when we returned home, I recall making a big Facebook announcement and told everyone that we had decided that our five-year plan was to pack up and move to the great state of North Carolina. Our friends were all asking, *"Oh, do you have family down there?"* The answer was, *"Nope. We don't know a single person down there, but we won't let that stop us. We're going to be living in NC in five years."*

Fast forward now to the year of 2022 and my husband was growing increasingly weary and we'll even say down right miserable because of his job. Unfortunately, it was one of the happiest years of my life because we had just wrapped up production on my last movie and was planning a red-carpet film premiere. (Yes, I'm an independent movie producer. That story possibly will come in another of April's beautiful books). Mark was so unhappy in his life and could not even fake being happy for me, which caused some resentment towards him on my part. He was working for a company called North American Lighting in Paris, Illinois as a Supervisor and working six days a week and twelve hours a day. He talked to me often about how bad things were getting. And while I had a great deal of sympathy for him, I also had so much on my plate. I felt like I already had a hundred different tasks to complete to get through my world premiere and seek distribution. I think eventually, he sensed the urgency I had to handle things in my own life and so he eventually bottled things up and held it all in, trying to relieve me of the extra stress.

Eventually I got through everything I had to do. We had an extremely successful premiere, I started submitting my film to dozens of film festivals and the awards started rolling in and I was sending the film out to various distributors, trying to get the film out. And while I was in a very happy place, things were not getting any better for my husband. NAL was such a horrible place to work that they could not keep decent help and that is the reason they worked their people seventy-two hours a week. Keep in mind a normal work week is forty hours a week. My husband and his people had to work seventy-two hours a week and then there was talk that they would have to start working on Sundays as well. Can you even imagine? I mean, everyone needs days off. Everyone needs time to rest. Everyone needs time with their families. This sort of thing is what tears families apart.

Things continued with no change throughout 2022. Now, it was January of 2023. My husband was angry. I was angry. He would often remind me that because it was such a horrible place to work, and they could not get locals to work there, the company began bussing illegals into town to work! With the illegals, came violence and drugs. One night in particular, the law had to be called on one of them. When the Police arrived and did a background check, they learned (and told my husband's Manager) that the man they came for actually had a warrant out for his arrest in Louisiana for attempted murder!

I had always been a praying wife. I always prayed for Mark's safety to and from work because of the incredibly dangerous way people drive, but I also prayed for him a ton because he was a man in a supervisory position. It was his job to write people up and even fire them. Never wanting anyone to retaliate against him for this, I prayed extra hard that no weapon formed against him would prosper (Isaiah 54:17). But now I had to *amp* up my prayers for a hedge of protection over him due to all the illegals that came in and started trouble at the plant. And I do not say this to be racist but it was the truth.

Over the course of a year, I had witnessed a real depression set in on my husband. His face said it all. I really believe his face showed him to have aged fifteen years in just the last six months. He was sad all the time. We argued a lot, and we had not previously been a couple who fought. He was taking his unhappiness out on me. I knew he didn't mean to, so I let it slide and just prayed extra hard for him. Before he would leave for work each day, I would hug him tightly and I could literally feel the stress within his entire body. I seriously felt like I was hugging a brick wall.

This man who once loved going to work and took great pride in his work became extremely sad, depressed, and dreaded having to make that drive from Indiana to Illinois six days a week. I did not know what else to do for him but to continue praying and I would pray longer and harder each day. I cried out to God, *"Please Lord, please make things change for Mark."* I begged Him for a miracle.

Things continued this way and on February 17, 2023, Mark texted me during his lunch break. He was truly broken. He said he truly did not know how much longer he could do this. And I texted him back with the words … *"Come Home."* He replied, *"What do you mean?"* And I responded, *"I mean, quit. Walk out the door and don't go back. Come home."* He could not believe his eyes. He questioned my response and said he could not quit. He had to have a job and I replied again, *"Quit now. Come home. God will provide. We will live off our savings until God opens a new door."* And he came home that night and when he walked into my waiting arms 40 minutes later he sobbed but it was cries of pure relief and joy. He told me how much it meant to him that I was allowing him to leave that horrible job. He said he was so blessed to have my love and support. He thanked me for several days after that for giving my blessing for him to quit. I said, *"How could I not? How many jobs have you given me your blessing to quit when I was miserable? What kind of wife would I be to expect you to stay there and be miserable beyond belief? Life is just too short."*

I told him we would be okay because God gave me peace about this. I told him that what we were doing was taking a big leap of faith, which God loves from His children. All we needed was faith the size of a mustard seed, and I had that. I told him to take a few weeks off to just relax and catch up on sleep before he started looking for a new job. When the time came for him to start looking for work again, he could not believe what I said to him next. I could have knocked him over with a feather when I told him, *"Honey, I think you need to start looking for work in North Carolina."* And his response was, *"Are you crazy? We can't afford to move to North Carolina right now when I'm out of work."* I replied to him, *"No, we can't afford to move, but I believe this is the word from God. I believe this is the time. You just start applying to jobs in NC that promise to relocate. And if it's truly God's will for us, He will make a way. He will open that door."*

But he still wasn't really sure. He said, *"Well, they can say they will relocate me, but why would they relocate me and spend all that money if they can just hire someone right there in their own town for nothing?"* I told him to stop being skeptical and just believe and have faith. And as the weeks passed by, I could literally see how "at peace" he had become after leaving NAL. I could tell the tension had left his body. When I hugged him it no longer felt like I was hugging a brick wall. He began to look younger again, no longer resembling an old man that I didn't recognize. The fighting between us had stopped. I saw the smile return to his face. He started joking again and making me laugh as he had always been able to do before. He was sleeping better and he had gotten his appetite back. This was the Mark I knew and loved all my adult life. And it made me so very happy.

He applied to dozens upon dozens of jobs in North Carolina. It didn't matter the region, as long as it was North Carolina, and he had the qualifications (manufacturing and supervisory experience) he would apply. He got several "initial phone call interviews" almost immediately but never got follow-up calls and he began to grow weary. I kept encouraging him to just "hold on and press forward."

One month turned into two months and still nothing, no job offers from North Carolina came in and he grew more discouraged. He would constantly ask me how we were doing financially, since I handled all of the finances. I would assure him that we were fine for about six more months using our savings. I would tell him to relax and just keep the faith. But then he hit his three-month mark with no job. This was a first for him and he was beside himself. It was now May 17, 2023. He could not take it any longer, so he started applying for jobs again in Terre Haute, where we lived, saying, "I just cannot go any longer without work. Maybe it's not in God's plan for us to move to North Carolina."

Secretly, I did not really want him applying for work in Terre Haute. I really believed we were meant to go to North Carolina, but at the same time, I had to respect his feelings about not having any job and not feeling like a man and a provider. I had to stand beside him and give him my blessing to look for work locally. But I prayed that a job offer from NC would roll in any day. I said, *"Lord, we both want your will for us. Lord, we both know that neither of us know what tomorrow holds, but You do and we want You to be completely in charge of our future. So let Your will be done and whatever it happens to be, we will accept it."*

Well it only took a week of applying for jobs in Terre Haute and boom! He had a job offer. To an outsider looking in, it appeared as if it was God's will for us to stay in Terre Haute and I remember being so very disappointed. I had, after all, told God that I would accept His will and obviously Mark had spent 3 whole months applying for work in North Carolina, with nothing to show for it. He applied for one week in Terre Haute and was offered a job. But to be honest, it was not a good job, it was simply a job. The salary was only half of what he had previously earned when he worked at NAL in Illinois and I really did not see how we were going to make it financially. But Mark was seemingly happy just to have been offered work again. I knew that if he accepted the position (and he said he was), that to make it, I was going to need to look for work as well, in spite of the fact he had always wanted me to be able to be a homemaker. But, you gotta do what you gotta do.

So Mark took the job offered to him and had stopped applying for work in North Carolina. He did say he would continue looking for better jobs locally but at least he had something until something better came along. And we settled in to the assumption that staying put was God's will for us even though we had been dreaming for fifteen years of moving to North Carolina.

But GOD!!

Mark had not even been on his new job for an entire week when he received a phone call interview from a company based out of Statesville, North Carolina. He had of course applied there before the Terre Haute job was offered. It just took them a little time to get around to calling him. The phone interview went very well and he was hopeful. But…. he had previously had several other "initial phone interviews" and nothing else became of them, so he did not want to get his hopes up only to be let down. And he went on about business as usual and went to work that night and the next night.

On Thursday, June 01, 2023, he was sitting on the front porch, as he did every day before going to his night shift job when he received a follow-up phone call from the job recruiter in NC. She told him that the company was so impressed with his qualifications and the results of the phone interview and they wanted to know if he would be willing to fly to NC for a face-to-face job interview on Monday, June 05. The only catch was that he would have to pay for the trip. If he was willing to put up the money, they wanted to set it up that day.

Without any hesitation whatsoever, he said, *"Yes Ma'am, I can be there!"* He hung up the phone and asked me to come to the porch and he was grinning from ear to ear when he told me he needed to make flight, hotel, and car reservations. He was on cloud nine. We went inside and together, we booked his flight for Sunday afternoon, along with his hotel and car and later, he went to his local night shift job with a spring in his step!

On Saturday, I received a text message from one of my dearest friends, Tracy. She invited me to attend church service with her the following day. We had stopped attending church after being incredibly hurt by our church and Pastor the previous year and had been having home-church ever since. Tracy attended a Mega church in Terre Haute and it was one I had promised myself I would never attend due to its "Mega" size but, I felt a nudge to say yes. So the following morning, as I was getting ready for church with my friend, Mark kissed me bye and made the one-hour drive to the Indianapolis airport. I remember telling him, *"Don't be nervous. You've got this."*

During the praise and worship portion of the service that morning, I was extremely moved. Even though I had loved home church over the past ten months, there was something so powerful about that worship and I was praying for God to bless Mark if, and only if it was His will. I told God that the six hundred dollars we had to invest for his one-day trip didn't mean a thing if He did not want us to pack up and move there. I totally surrendered what I wanted and what Mark wanted and just kept repeating to the Lord, *"We want Your will for our lives God, Yours and Yours alone."* And suddenly the Lord spoke to me so loud and so clearly, like He had never done before. He said, *"My child, I am about to move mountains for you and for Mark! I cannot wait until you both see what I am about to do in your lives. Get ready for I am going to bless you beyond what you can even imagine!"*

And I'm telling you, I began to weep like a new born baby. I could not control anything! I quickly began to thank Him, and praise Him for this word. At the same time, I was also trying desperately to find the nearest tissue box to catch the you know what falling from my nose and pouring from my dark brown eyes. I was quite literally a mess, but it was a beautiful kind of mess as I was the daughter of the King of Kings, accepting an amazing gift from my Father in Heaven! Halleluiah.

When church was dismissed, I disclosed to my friend Tracy that the Lord gave me clarification that Mark was going to be offered that job and we would soon be moving to North Carolina. She embraced me and started to cry. She was happy for us because she knew it was our dream, but didn't want to lose me. That afternoon, when Mark got checked into his hotel and called me, I informed him of what God told me in church that morning. I said, *"Be ready honey. You're going to be offered that job, God said so."*

On Monday, when he got out of the interview, he phoned me to tell me he felt really good and he thought it went really well. Then he headed to the airport and he was home that night. The very next day they called him and said, *"We didn't want to waste any time and take a chance of losing you. We want you at Denso!"*

And it got even better. The relocation package was out of this world! The minute he accepted the position, they initiated a deposit of five thousand dollars into our checking account! It was to be used for anything we needed, no questions asked! (Only GOD!) Also, we were assigned a case manager by the name of Nadine. Everything was to go through her. She would handle everything. In addition, the company hired Joyce Vanlines and they would be in charge of coming to our home and packing up everything we owned and driving it to NC. And eventually, once we got there, they would also come and deliver all our things and even unpack for us (if I wanted them to, which I opted out of).

The company (Denso) sent us a real estate agent to put our home on the market. They assigned us another real estate agent in NC to help us find our new home! And the best part was that the company was going to pay all of our closing costs (which ended up being around fifteen thousand dollars!) Additionally, they paid all commission fees for both realtors. They wanted Mark to start his new position on July 10th and were putting him up in one of the finest hotels in town at their expense. And, once we got an acceptable offer on our home, they were going to pay to send me out to NC for 7 days to house hunt. My flight, lodging and per diem were all to be covered by the relocation package. And there were additional blessings attached as well. The total price tag of this relocation package was a whopping seventy-five thousand dollars!

Again, I say to you --- ONLY GOD could have orchestrated such amazing blessings!

By the time everything got in order, our Terre Haute agent got our home listed on July 05. Mark had to head out on July 08 so he could begin his new dream job on July 10th. We missed each other like crazy but we knew a short separation was inevitable in order to make our fifteen- year long dream a reality.

North Carolina seems to be where a lot of folks dream of living. I say that because the demand for homes here are very high and listed homes barely lasted a few days on the market. There was no reason for me to fly out and house hunt until we received a Bonafide offer on our home, but that didn't stop Mark from going out several evenings a week after working to look at potential homes. He would do video chats so I could see what he saw. I was so proud of him. The hardest part about me having to get out of our home and let the agent show it was having to get our three fur babies out and keep them cooped up in a hot car for only God knew how long. They absolutely hated it and I hated it for them.

With every showing, I prayed that GOD would send someone who would love our house and want it. And it only took a month to get a <u>cash offer</u> and then four more weeks to close! Mark came back from North Carolina on September fourth and made some rounds to say his final goodbyes to friends and family and we made our final drive out of Indiana exactly eight weeks after our home went on the market.

We had purchased our Terre Haute home in 2016 and had been quite happy here in this home. We built a lot of memories and saw a lot of good times and a few bad. We filmed one of our movies entirely in this home and filmed two more partially in this home, so the house will always live forever in my heart through my movies. When it was all said and done, we sold the house and walked away with an astonishing seventy-five thousand dollars in equity that would come in very handy as a down payment on our new home.

And once again, I must testify: Only GOD could have orchestrated that.

Please allow me to quickly go a little off subject of NC to demonstrate how big of a mountain GOD moved for Mark and me. So I just previously mentioned above that we had purchased our Terre Haute home in 2016. But before that, we attempted to purchase a home in 2013, priced at one hundred and fifty-five thousand dollars. We had previously filed bankruptcy in 2011 and so in 2013 we of course was denied a bank loan to purchase for $155,000 but thankfully, the owners of the home decided to rent the home to us because they wanted to move to Florida and needed someone in the home, so it all worked out.

But I say that to say this. In 2013, our credit was only in the mid five hundreds (probably mostly due to the bankruptcy) which I am certainly not proud of, but mounting medical bills forced us into it. And in 2016 when we wanted to buy our Royce Drive home in Terre Haute, the bank would only approve us for ninety thousand dollars. Thankfully, we put in an offer for ninety thousand and it was accepted.

But GOD!!

When we sold our Royse Drive home last year to come to North Carolina, our home sold for seventy-five thousand dollars <u>more</u> than what we paid for it just seven years prior, and we had not done any re-modeling other than painting a few of the rooms. Only God could have orchestrated that.

And when it came time to get a bank loan in North Carolina, we were absolutely amazed to learn that both Mark's and my credit scores had risen from the five hundred range to the high 800's. WOW! And we were immediately approved for three hundred and fifty-thousand dollars. And we were told that once we began to shop around, if we needed more, to "let them know" and they would approve us for more. What's really astonishing also is that Mark had been unemployed for three whole months before being offered the job in NC and still the bank was willing to loan us this much for a home!

Only GOD!!

Remember, in 2016, we could only purchase a home for no more than ninety thousand. That is the kind of miracles that our GOD will give to His children. He wants to bless us if what we are seeking lines up with His will. Amen!

Despite Mark interviewing with Denso in their Statesville location, they actually wanted him at their Salisbury location. And because we could not find a home in Salisbury, we ended up having to purchase a home in Winston Salem. I'll be completely honest, this is *not* where we thought we would end up, nor is it where we wanted to end up. We are *small town folks* and originally started our married life in the tiny town of Clinton, Indiana, with a population of less than five thousand. After twenty-five years of marriage, we moved to Terre Haute, which had a population of roughly sixty thousand. So, of course I am quite intimidated by Winston Salem's massive population of more than five hundred thousand. I can't even begin to explain what driving here does to my nerves. But this is where the house is that God provided. So, we make the best of it and thank Him for it.

What we love most about where we are now is the weather! Oh yes, it is very hot. But we all agree we'll take the heat over the extreme cold that Indiana dishes out every winter. We know that this is the new life GOD blessed us with. We asked for it for fifteen years and while NC is a great deal more expensive than Indiana, we like it and are making the most of it.

Mark loves his job. He works a straight eight hours a day, (instead of twelve hours like he did at NAL) occasionally he works a

Saturday, but he doesn't mind because thankfully he is paid for his additional time at work. Last month he got a fabulous bonus and a pay raise! (Thank you Jesus) He just recently purchased a boat and a membership to a lake where he can go fishing anytime he wants. Fishing has been one of his deepest loves for his entire life.

We are back in church again and we found the absolute greatest Veterinarian for our fur babies. And I am finally comfortable driving to all the places I need to drive to, which is a huge blessing. And we are only a forty-five-minute drive to Mount Airy, NC (Mayberry). We went there to celebrate my birthday last year and again this past April for our wedding anniversary and plan to take our son Christopher for his birthday next month.

Because Denso did so much for us with the relocation package and because we had such great equity when we sold our home, we are in the absolute best financial shape we have ever been in and we've been married for thirty-six years. So if I had to say one thing it would be that moving here truly put us in a great place financially, despite the fact that the cost of living in NC is a lot higher than it is in Indiana. And financial freedom is an incredible blessing. With financial freedom comes a peace of mind that I would not trade for anything.

And…we are only four hours from the beach. Mark truly comes alive when he is standing on and looking out at the ocean. And me? I go to the ocean to nap! There's something so magnificent about lying on the warm sand and listening to the waves, thinking, *"God created this beauty for us! Oh how amazing is He to give us something so powerful, mysterious, and awesome to enjoy? Life is good and GOD is GREAT!"*

I hope you've been inspired and blessed by our story of how our dream became a reality in God's perfect timing and it only took fifteen years!

Here are a few of my favorite scriptures that line up with our testimony. I hope you too will find them comforting during your challenging seasons.

Scripture Share

He is able to do exceedingly and abundantly above all that we ask or think, according to the power that works in us, to Him be the glory.
-(Ephesians 3:20)

"Ask and it will be given to you; seek and you will find; knock and the door will be opened to you."
-(Matthew 7:7)

Jesus replied, "Truly I tell you, if you have faith as small as a mustard seed, you can say to this mountain, 'Move from here to there,' and it will move. Nothing will be impossible for you."
-(Matthew 17:20)

I'd like to leave you with these final words…

Encouragement

The moment God the Father put a dream in your / my heart, the moment the promise took root, He not only started it, but He also set a completion date. God is called the Author and the Finisher of our faith. He would not have given you / us the dream and the promise would not have come alive if He didn't already have a plan to bring it to pass. He will not endorse anything that is contrary to His word.

If you would like to connect with me, I'd love to hear from you. I can be reached at: candy_dreamscometruefilmsllc@yahoo.com

Be forever blessed! Candy

✝

Two of my movies, "THE TEXT" and "A Second Chance" can be viewed on Tubi for free. Praise Jesus-both are multi-award winning, Christian films and are intended to inspire our audiences.

Candy Beard Films-

Vanished - premiered & released on DVD in 2014.

Cries Unheard & **My Mother's Replacement** - premiered & released on DVD in 2015

The Promise - premiered & released on DVD in 2017.

A Second Chance - premiered & released on DVD in 2018
*But officially got worldwide distribution in August 2024.

The Text - premiered in June 2022, released on DVD in Dec. 2023
*But officially got worldwide distribution in July 2024.

NEW BEGINNINGS
Shirley Rainwater

*For I know the plans I have for you,
declares the Lord, plans to prosper you and not to
harm you, plans to give you hope and a future.*
             -(Jeremiah 29:11, NIV)

My youngest son lives in Arkansas and had worked in construction for many years when he decided to start flipping houses...

One day he was out looking for his next project when he came upon an old, dilapidated house that hadn't been lived in for years. He liked the little cottage, and felt very drawn to it. He could see in his mind what it could be, with hard work and love. So instead of fixing it up to sell, he decided to keep it for himself. He was so excited when he called to tell me about his latest find. He knew I would love it because there was a little white church directly across the street from the house. He sent pictures of the church with its steeple and white siding; looking like something out of Little House on the Prairie.

Previously Troy had said he had been halfheartedly looking for a church home for the last year or so, but nothing seemed to "fit." We talked about it many times. The funny thing to me was that now God planted him right across the street from a church! I suggested he try visiting it sometime. It took months, but little by little he took that old, abandoned house and made it into a home. He was happy with the way it turned out. He told me he liked to sit out on the front porch and listen to the music from the church across the street. At night, the light from the windows inside the church would shine like a warm beacon.

On the following Sunday he wandered across the street to check it out and attend services.. It was a small church and he was welcomed by the Pastor and the congregation. They were delighted to meet the person who was fixing up the neighborhood eyesore. They were full of lots of questions for him.

Troy had recently met a nice woman and before long they were going to the church on a regular basis. When it was announced that they needed help with the Pantry Ministry gathering and putting together boxes of food for the needy folks in the neighborhood,

Troy and Kristy volunteered to help. One Sunday, not long after, the Pastor asked them stand up during services and he thanked them for saving the Pantry, because before they came to the church, they were just about to shut it down for lack of volunteers. Troy said it felt really good to be able to help. He said it made them feel like they belonged there.

A few weeks later one of the men from the church came over to the house and asked if he would be willing to remodel the old, outdated restroom and make it ADA (American Disabilities Act) compliant. Troy was surprised, but said he'd be glad to do it.

He felt that that was his *calling in life*, building things...

and Troy felt right at home doing it. For a long time we had been talking about how he could serve the Lord should the opportunity ever arise. Here was his chance.

God led him there…

They *needed* him there…

And Troy needed a church home…

I believe Troy listened to his heart when [9]God led him to that forlorn little house that nobody wanted, and my son finally found a church home and a new beginning.

Scripture Share

"Thy word is a lamp unto my feet and a light unto my path"

-(Psalm 119:105, KJV)

---

[9] *Proverbs 16:9: "We can make our plans, but the Lord determines our steps"*

Encouragement

I believe that God speaks to us in many ways. At times He whispers in our ear or calls our attention to something. Other times He guides our eyes to things *He wants us to see*. At times He may peak our interest if only we would pay attention. Occasionally He speaks to us through other people…

I have this "thing" I always try to do.

When I hear something once, I might ignore it.

If I hear something twice, I *notice* it.

When I hear that "something" for the third time, I *pay attention* because *the Lord* might be trying to tell me something I *need* to know or do…

Just today, the Lord helped when I was grocery shopping. I was standing in the store almost ready to check out, but knowing I was forgetting something on my list at home. But for the life of me, I couldn't remember what it was. So I stopped and prayed, and instantaneously I knew it was "blueberry waffles!" I know that sounds silly, but when I keep my mind and eyes on the Lord, He has shown me that He cares about even the *littlest things*. He tells us to come to Him with our prayers and supplications. If only we can remember to be quiet so that we can hear Him whispering in our ear.

      Love & Blessings to You Always,

Shirley Rainwater

WHY LORD, WHY
Nancy J. Stoll

It was the decade of the 70's when I graduated from college and entered my first career in the man's world of corporate "Big Box Family Center" retail. Sure there were tons of women out on the sales floor "taking care of business and getting the job done" but men were the ones managing the operations of it all.

I had *always* envisioned myself as a business leader.

Therefore, as I entered the arena, my goal was two-fold; to learn a game my mother never taught me - "The Game of Business" and to become one of those women who broke glass ceilings. Proof that my retail career was on the fast track came as time passed. I progressed through the ranks of department head, three in-store management positions, and finally was promoted to Lead Co-Manager. I was now second in command and only two steps away from reaching my ultimate goal of being promoted to General Manager (GM) of a Family Center Store.

Supervision of all department heads, purchasing for the entire store, the layout and set-up of all seasonal counter and feature displays, and new employee training were all my responsibilities. I loved what I was doing and it became my life's focus. However, as in any job, there were things I didn't like. I disliked training the former retail managers hired from other companies. I seriously and truly disliked it with great passion. (That's my phrase for the word "Hate!)

These "new hires" were all men and were given "Manager-in-Training" titles. I was the store's Lead Co-Manager and their female trainer. I showed them the ropes, detailed the company's operational policies and procedures, and assured that they knew and understood all the company's "And this is how we do it!" factors. However, reality soon set in. These men I trained were on a faster promotional track than me and that caused me many agonizing tears as I cried, "*Why, Lord, why?*"

They would get promoted to the Five and Dime General Store GM positions. If they proved themselves capable there, it would later lead to being promoted back into a Family Center as GM. That's what I wanted to happen to me! However, I was always be *overlooked.*

I would fake happiness for them but sit in my office silently crying, praying, "*Why God, why?*

How am I ever going to become a Family Center GM?" I would receive no answer from Him as I prayed. My heart broke every time it happened and continued to cry, "Why?"[10] However, I didn't know God would soon teach me an unforgettable lesson and give me my answer.

Breaking news came down from corporate headquarters several months after my last bout of crying "*Why God, why*".

---

[10] *Philippian's 4:19, ESV - And my God will supply every need of yours according to his riches in glory in Christ Jesus.*

The new CEO was boldly taking charge of the corporate reins. Major and significant changes were being immediately implemented. The most critical change was the operational structure of the *entire* company. The smaller General Store and the larger Family Center operations would become separate retail divisions. Each division would have its own realigned and defined regions, districts, and management structures. There would be *no* mingling nor joint management oversight between the two divisions. Plus, are you ready for this? All existing management personnel would remain in their present divisional positions *without* the opportunity to be transferred from or promoted into the other retail division's management structure.

In other words, if I had been promoted to GM of a smaller General Store I would have been stuck in that position without the possibility of ever obtaining a Family Center GM position and vice versa.

Oh, my gosh! I was praising God that I hadn't gotten those promotions!

I *wanted* a management career in the Family Centers, not the General Stores. I would have been stuck in something I didn't want.[11] God went before me. He knew what was to come, and He handled it all. That was His answer to my cries of "Why?" and I rejoiced in His answer.

The other thing I didn't like about my Co-Manager position was based on something I loved to do, which led me to yet another cry of "*Why Lord, why?*"

I loved designing, developing, and setting up seasonal counters and feature displays. Once set, I would propose the display layouts to the regional office. Many of them were adopted region wide. However, it was so frustrating when the Regional Vice President (VP) loved and approved it, but then my District Manager (DM) wouldn't like it and would always tell me to change it. Then, after changing it, the Regional VP would see the change and say, "Why in the heck did you change it? Change it back!" It was like

---

[11] *Jeremiah 29:11, NIV- For I know the plans I have for you, declares the Lord, "to prosper you and not to harm, you plans to give you a hope and a future."*

being caught in the middle of a battle between those above me. They were all wasting my time and my payroll. With that, my entrepreneurial spirit kicked in full force. I started to think I could do this better on my own.

I attended several Small Business Administration (SBA) Business Start-up Workshops. I learned what it would take and how to start a business, what was available and what to do if I needed a loan, and what the SBA provided to help make it all happen.

At that time, the SBA had a loan program called "The Direct Loan Program." It was a "targeted market" loan program that provided low-interest loan assistance directly from the SBA to women, minorities, and the handicapped population. This loan program offered an unprecedented three percent interest rate in a world where commercial loan rates were well above nineteen percent. The only catch was you had to take your business plan to the bank and the bank had to tell you "No." If that were the case, the applicant could take their business plan and the bank's "Letter of Reasoning" explaining why they said "No" directly to the SBA and request the SBA to "directly" fund the business endeavor.

Please note this SBA loan program doesn't exist anymore but at the time, I was praising *God*...it did!

I thought my chances of getting this loan were great because I met two of the qualifications. I'm a woman, and believe it or not, I'm considered to be legally handicapped. I jokingly tell people, "It's not my brain. It's my foot!" I was born with a clubfoot, but thanks to multiple major surgeries and therapy sessions during the first six years of my life, I can walk, run, and dance almost like anybody. And now, my "physical defect" might help me get a loan.

I did my research, applied my business knowledge, and developed my business plan to establish a small retail boutique. It took months of hard work to create the plan and the financial projections for both the SBA's three percent interest loan and the bank's nineteen percent interest loan.

Finally completed, I took it to the bank, praying they would say "No," but they said "Yes." I was discouraged but still wanted to do it. That is until I got home and seriously reviewed the nineteen-percent financial projections. The revenues I needed to meet monthly fixed expenses were sky-high. It would take an outrageously long time to pay off the loan and drastically impact the lifestyle my family and I had become accustomed to living. The next morning, I called the bank and declined their loan offer. This decision was not based on doubt in my desire or abilities. It was based on something I found more valuable…

Earlier that year, my husband and I took our first-ever vacation without our daughter. It was a wonderful two-week, ocean-front condo getaway vacation to the St. Thomas Virgin Islands. The memories of sitting on our balcony, drinking my morning coffee, watching the sunrise as the cruise ships pulled into port, and saying to myself, "Oh, yeah, I deserve this," were still fresh in my mind. A review of my projections showed it would take at least ten years before we could even seriously think about returning to St. Thomas. My brain screamed, "No way!" and that's the reason I declined the loan.

For weeks I angrily cried, asking the Lord why He had let me do all this hard business start-up work and planning for nothing.

His answer to that "*Why*" would not come for almost four years as [12]He, unknowingly to me, went before me preparing me for the plan He had in store for me. And, let me tell you, during those years there were many other cries of "*Why Lord Why?*"

Shortly after being promoted to GM of a 40,000 sq. ft. Family Center, the company I worked for was bought out by a large Five and Dime retailer. Their largest stores were no bigger than 15,000 sq. ft. Therefore, my 40,000 sq. ft. store was closed.

" *Why Lord? Why?!*"

Under the new company, I thought I'd be transferred to one of my former employer's smaller stores. However, due to my proven

---

[12] *Deuteronomy 31:8, NLT- Do not be afraid or discouraged, for the Lord will personally go ahead of you. He will be with you; he will neither fail you nor abandon you.*

counter layout and merchandising experience, the new company *promoted* me to Regional Relay Merchandising Manager.

My team and I traveled the region relaying my former employer's smaller stores. We also trained all store personnel in the new company way and prepared them to pass their mandatory "Grand Reopening Corporate Review."

I loved what I was doing but I was never home and when I was, I lived out of my suitcase. This was extremely hard on me, my marriage, and my family. Cries of "Why" were replaced with asking the Lord to help me.

As time passed and to save my marriage, I resigned from my regional position and requested to be reassigned as a store GM. My husband and I thought the store would be close to where we lived. However, instead of being close it was hundreds of miles away in Indiana and the company needed me there A.S.A.P. We had to move. My husband gave up his job to try and find one after we moved, and our shy daughter had to leave all her long-time friends behind.

My *"Why Lord? Why?!"* cries were angrily shouted up to God.

Home life settled to somewhat normal once the move was complete. However, the store I was assigned to was anything but normal and complete. I couldn't believe the store had passed its Corporate Review. I later found out that both the former GM and the assistant manager had quit two weeks earlier and left their mess behind. I was promised an assistant manager but that never came to pass. Much needed to be done and everything was on my shoulders.

"Why Lord Why"

Being the "Take Control" person I was at the time, that's exactly what I did. I took control! Over the following twelve months my "Why Lord Why" cries multiplied as I worked myself to death seven days a week fourteen hours a day, survived several horrific devastating in-store disasters, and it all finally took its toll. I won't go into detail, but burnout is no laughing matter.

It happened the Wednesday before Thanksgiving. I crashed, burned, and experienced a total emotional and physical breakdown. It was terrible and my tears were flowing down my face like a river. I called Corporate Headquarters. In tears, told them I quit, my keys would be on my desk ready for the new GM to take charge, my lead "Key-carrier" employee would open the store on Friday to kick off the Holiday Shopping season, and welcome the store's new GM into the store.

Now, ya wanna talk about *"Why Lord, Why?!"* cries?..

I had just lost *everything* I'd ever worked for! Oh, they were there big and strong! However, thanks to my entire Christ-centered family, that Thanksgiving and Christmas season was the best I had experienced in years.

During the following three months, I focused all my energies on recovering as my family showered me with their compassionate love and prayers. Let me tell you, there's power in both of those things. By the end of the third month, I had responded to an

Executive position posted in the local newspaper, by a regional Chamber of Commerce.. It didn't specifically say what the position was but I knew I held everything they were looking for. I had experience in business operations, employee management, marketing, AND small business start-up efforts, business planning, along with bank and SBA business loan processes!

Interviews were held and shortly thereafter I became the first Executive Director of the East Central Indiana Small Business Development Center (ECSBDC). It was only then that I got my answer to all of my *"Why Lord?... Why?"* questions. Throughout all of my *"Why* cries" the good Lord was simply going before me and preparing me for the perfect plan He had for my life and it came at the perfect time!

My Dear Friends,
As You Move Forward in Your Life,
Remember these words from GOD!

Scripture Share
*In their hearts, humans plan their course,
but the Lord establishes their steps.*
-(Proverbs 16:9, NIV)

For I know the plans I have for you," declares the LORD, "plans to prosper you and not to harm you, plans to give you hope and a future.
-(Jeremiah 29:11, NIV)

Do not be afraid or discouraged, for the Lord will personally go ahead of you. He will be with you; he will neither fail you nor abandon you.
-(Deuteronomy 31:8, NLT)

Trust in the Lord with all your heart and lean not on your own understanding; in all your ways submit and acknowledge him, and he will make your paths straight.
-(Proverbs 3:5-6, NIV)

BECAUSE

We know that God causes everything to work together for the good of those who love God and are called according to his purpose for them.
-(Romans 8:28, NIV)

I can do all this through Christ who strengthens me!
-(Philippians 4:13, NKJV)

AND YES YOU CAN!

But never forget, it is *through Him* who strengthens you

-that YOU CAN!!

Encouragement

There's nothing wrong with asking God, "Why?" Even great King David struggled and asked the Lord that question. But just as King David did, we must realize that God holds the answers and knows the best time to reveal them. If He immediately gave us the answer to our "Why?, we probably wouldn't understand it anyhow because we would be too caught up in the circumstances that caused our "Why?" However, in time, God does and will provide the answer. His answer may come immediately, but usually, it comes as we look back and realize how He was working through and within our circumstances. Years ago, there was a TV show called "Father Knows Best." In every episode, the father showed that he knew how and when to take care of every situation, solve every problem, answer every question, heal every hurt, comfort, and lovingly care for those he loved in his life. This father was a fictitious character.

Our Heavenly Father God is not fictional. He's rock-solidly real and all-powerful! He holds all the knowledge, know-how, and when best to make things happen. Believe it when He says His ways are not our ways and His timing is perfect! Be patient and add another question to ask of Him. Ask, "Lord, what are you trying to teach me?" He will eventually show you and give you the answers to your "Why" and "What" questions. How do I know? Because He has proven to me throughout my life that His timing, purpose, and loving hands are all and always at work preparing and leading us toward a future we don't even know exists.

He's a man of His word! Trust Him in all things and get ready to be blown away by His grace, love, and abilities that are all far above ours!

From the Opened Eyes of My Heart
To Yours

Nancy J. Stoll

✝

WALK BY FAITH
Sue Rakoczy

January 27th, 2012,

It was a day that started out just like any other…

I let the dogs out, grabbed my keys, and tied my shoes, for the very last time. (what I didn't know then.) I wouldn't come home again until May 5th.

I had suffered a massive stroke at 2:45 PM while I was at work, talking with a co-worker. I was in the hospital half paralyzed by 3:00 PM. *Fifteen minutes*, that my world would be turned upside down, or maybe right side up. I had to learn to walk again and soon began looking for reasons why this had happened to me. There was no medical explanation.

I walked by the faith that I *didn't* even know I had yet.

I always felt, even on the darkest days, that I was walking towards something. While I was in New York, I told my teacher in Ohio that I would come back carrying all the love in the world. In retrospect., It seemed like I was walking toward a relationship with God. I continue going to services and getting involved. I quelled my doubts and misgivings with reading., research, long talks with Christians I respected and an earnest openness to see what others seem to see.

One day I had a deep-knowing, a feeling. That there was nothing not aligned with God. Since that day, I have a growing, appreciation, and awareness, of how God is woven into all things. And how If you look for God, you will see God.

However, I wasn't looking too much before my stroke. I was *busy* with work and life. It's hard calling the stroke a blessing, but in many ways, it was. I really miss using my arm and hiking, but it was the stroke, that God used to give me time to address deeper questions. It also stripped me of the illusionary sense of control and self-sufficiency. I couldn't even take care of myself. My family really showed up for me as my church family does now. I think of Jesus's birth now with an awe that God would come as a vulnerable., helpless baby, that would someday save the world and be our bridge to the infinite. I couldn't see any of this until God was my only hope.

My Prayer -God, may I always have the faith to walk through dark days and hope to withstand the trials and tribulations. May they serve to draw me closer to you. Thank you, Lord, for what you help me endure and for giving me strength for this struggle. Amen.

Scripture share

[7] for we walk by faith, not by sight.

-(2 Corinthians 5:7, ESV)

Encouragement

Keep going, there's always more- biggest lesson for me has been there is always more ways to embrace God, intellectually, emotionally, and personally. A friend once told me a C.S. Lewis quote, I like- "If the intention to walk is there, God is pleased even with our stumbles. And from someone else, "If you find yourself judging your faith, focus instead on Jesus." Just Keep going.

God Bless your efforts,

Sue

FROM BROKEN TO BEAUTIFUL
Dawn Hoskins

This is my story, from broken to beautiful- how Art & Faith, brought me back to life...

I was born into a world that seemed designed to break me. From the moment I could understand words, I was told that I was a mistake, a burden no one wanted. In my family, love was a foreign concept. What I did know was abuse, both physical and emotional. I was told I was worthless, and the cruelty I endured convinced me that it was true.

For years, I lived in a world where pain was normal, where violence was the language spoken behind closed doors. I thought every family was like mine, that this was just the way life was. Growing up in that environment, I became numb to the idea of hope or love. The idea of God was laughable to me. How could a benevolent deity exist in a world where a child could suffer so much? I saw no evidence of divine intervention in my life; all I saw was darkness. And so, I declared myself an atheist

If there was a God, I thought, He had abandoned me long ago.

As I grew older, I carried the scars of my childhood into every relationship. I didn't know what love looked like; all I knew was abuse. So, I continued to seek out partners who treated me the way I had been treated all my life—badly. One abusive relationship followed another, each one a twisted reflection of the home I had grown up in. It was as if I was on a relentless quest to confirm what I had been taught: that I was unworthy of kindness, of love, of happiness.

My last relationship almost ended me. The abuse escalated until, one horrific night, it reached its climax. I was beaten so severely that my body could no longer bear the pain. I remember the darkness closing in, the sensation of my life slipping away. I was later told that I *died* that night, that my heart stopped. In that moment between life and death, something extraordinary happened—something that shattered my disbelief. In the cold, sterile light of the hospital room, I saw them—two large, radiant angels standing silently at the foot of my bed. They didn't speak, but somehow, I could hear them clearly in my mind. They told me I would be okay, that it wasn't my time to go. They said, "I had a purpose to fulfill." For the first time in my life, I felt peace. It was as if they were pouring their light into the deepest, darkest parts of my soul. I came back from that brink, not just to life, but to a new understanding.

I knew then that *God was real*, that He had never abandoned me, even when I had abandoned hope in Him.

But surviving was only the *beginning*. My body was broken. In the months and years that followed, I underwent over twenty-surgeries, including two reconstructive surgeries on my face. The physical pain was excruciating, but it was nothing compared to the emotional and spiritual pain I had carried for so long. My body had to be rebuilt, piece by piece, and so did my spirit. The surgeries left me with scars, disabilities, and chronic health issues that I still struggle with every day. But they also left me with something else—a will to live, to fight, to prove that I was more than the sum of what had been done to me.

Soon a talent that the Lord had given me long before I knew Him, would begin to manifest.

As I began the long process of healing, I found myself drawn to art. I had never been an artist, never picked up a paintbrush in my life, but something inside me needed to create. I started painting as a way to release the turmoil inside me. Each stroke of the brush was a scream, a sob, a release of the emotions I had locked away for so long. I poured my pain, my anger, my hope onto every canvas. Art became my therapy, my voice when words were inadequate. Through art, I began to understand myself in ways I never had before. I realized that every piece I created was a reflection of my journey—a piece of my soul laid bare for the world to see. It was as if I was reclaiming my story, transforming the narrative of my life from one of suffering to one of resilience and hope. With every painting, I felt a little more of the darkness lift.

Art was not just an outlet; it was a bridge to *God,* a way to feel His Presence and His love for me.

It was in this creative process that I found my true calling. I wanted to share this healing power of art with others. I wanted to show people that no matter how broken they felt, no matter how many scars they carried—inside or out—there was beauty within them waiting to be expressed. This desire led to the birth of my art and design business, "Creative Soul Art & Design." I refused to let my disabilities, or my past define what I could achieve. I was determined to create things that were unique and inspiring, to use my story to bring hope to others.

Today, I pour my heart and soul into every piece I create, whether it's a painting, a shirt design, or any other medium that captures my imagination. Each creation is a testament to my journey, a piece of my soul that says, "I survived. I am still here." It is my mission to inspire others through my work, to let them see that healing is possible, that they too can overcome whatever darkness they face. Through "Creative Soul Art & Design," I aim to spread a message of resilience, hope, and the transformative power of creativity.

Starting and running a business is not easy, especially with the health challenges I face. Some days, the pain is unbearable, and the limitations of my body remind me of all that I have been through. But I refuse to let that stop me. I have learned to adapt, to find new ways to create even on the days when I can barely move. My disabilities are part of my story, but they do not define my potential. If anything, they fuel my determination to show the world that beauty and strength can emerge from the most broken places.

I know now, without a shadow of a doubt, that *God* is with me.

He was there in the hospital room, sending His angels to bring me back to life. He is with me in every brushstroke, in every design, in every moment when I feel too weak to go on but find the strength to keep pushing forward. My life is not perfect, and my journey is far from over, but I am no longer the person who believed they were a mistake. I am a survivor, an artist, a child of God with a purpose.

Breathe... It's just a chapter, not the whole story. Life's struggles are not the entirety of who we are—they're just moments in the masterpiece God is crafting within us. Each challenge we face is like a steep climb on a hike: hard and demanding in the moment, yet it leads to a rewarding view at the top.

Scripture Share

Psalm 121:1-2 reminds us: *"I lift up my eyes to the mountains—where does my help come from? My help comes from the Lord, the Maker of heaven and earth."*

Every mountain we climb teaches us perseverance, and every sunset is God's promise of new beginnings. As we walk through life's journey, let's remember the truth of ...

Romans 8:28: *"And we know that in all things God works for the good of those who love him, who have been called according to his purpose."*

Keep turning the pages of your story, it's filled with hope and resilience waiting to unfold. Let's cherish the journey, the lessons, and the growth along the way. Together, we are stronger. Keep going, for the best is yet to come! Trust in God's faithfulness and know that He is writing a story of beauty and purpose in you.

Encouragement

To anyone who feels trapped in darkness, who thinks they are too broken to ever be whole again, I want to say this: Your story is not over. There is light on the other side of your pain. You are not alone, and you are not without hope. Your life can change, and even with disabilities or scars—whether seen or unseen—God can create something beautiful. You can fulfill your dreams.

Through art, I found my voice and my purpose. Through faith, I found my strength. And through **"Creative Soul Art & Design,"** I am living proof that out of the ashes, a new creation can rise. This is my journey, my testimony. It is not just about overcoming abuse or surviving near death; it's about finding a way to turn the broken pieces of my life into something beautiful, something that speaks of resilience and hope. It's about knowing that every stroke of my brush, every design I create, is a declaration that I am still here, that I matter, and that so do you.

The power of God's Transformative love changed my life. I transformed from a state of complete brokenness into a testament of strength and beauty. The word brokenness can sound intimidating—like something to fear. But in God's hands, brokenness is not about shattering us to pieces; it's about gently breaking the outer shell that keeps us from experiencing the fullness of His love and purpose. God's desire isn't to break our spirits but to break away the pride, rebellion, selfishness, and independence that separate us from Him. He knows that when we rely on ourselves, we miss out on the incredible power and grace

He wants to work *in* and *through* us.

Psalm 51:17, says: *"The sacrifices of God are a broken spirit; a broken and contrite heart, O God, you will not despise."*

A heart- broken before God isn't weak; it's surrendered. It's open and ready for His transforming love to take root and grow. Think of brokenness as the tender hands of a gardener cracking open a seed's hard shell so new life can emerge. In the same way,

God's love doesn't harm us—it heals us. He uses our struggles, our suffering, and even our failures to shape us into the people He created us to be. So don't fear brokenness—see it as God's refining work. With each layer He breaks away, His love draws us closer, revealing our true purpose in Him. Through the breaking, we grow; through the surrender, we find freedom; and in His transformative love, we become whole. Trust in his process and know that brokenness *is not the end*—it's the beginning of a new, beautiful chapter of growth and purpose.

Beauty from Ashes-

Dawn

✝

A FINAL NOTE FROM APRIL YARBER

To our beautiful Readers--

Thank you all once again for joining us on this journey through Volume Three. I pray you experienced the power of love from our Lord Jesus Christ, as you were reading through these miraculous stories. I also pray that you felt the love offered by our contributors for **YOU**. As they shared their words of encouragement and their personal stories with the hopes that they could touch just one heart, help just one person. Thats what *Jesus* does, He goes after the *one*. Also to **our readers**, thank you for opening your hearts to this series.

A Special Thanks to **our contributors**, your bravery in sharing your stories is a true act of love.

I am deeply grateful for each of you. ***Together***, we are reminded of the incredible power of faith and the love that connects us all through Christ.

If you enjoyed this series, we ask you to please **kindly review** on any book sites where reviews are welcome. This will provide feedback to others in search of books worthy of reading. Helping us get the word out by creating interest in this series. The goal is to reach more people with the love of Jesus.

Showing others who He is, by the telling of our stories

My Prayer and my hope for this series is that The Lord Jesus use it to help build His Kingdom.

All for His Glory.

OTHER GOOD WORKS CONTRIBUTORS PAGE

April S. Yarber- Berg
GOD ALWAYS FULFILLS HIS PURPOSE
Award Winning -Author, Speaker, Series Developer and Contributor- story one. Speaking to the Heart Publishing Owner.
Author: **Speaking to the Heart Daily Devotions, Moments with Jesus.** Trilogy Publishing, *Published, 2019.*
Speaking to the Heart from Flicker to Flame, anthology book series: Speaking to the Heart Publishing. Volume One- Published *2021.Second* edition published *2024*
Volume Two- *Published 2023*
Email- *Speakingtothehearts@gmail.com*

Sharyn Hernandez
EVERYONE WHO CALLS ON HIS NAME
Speaker, Series Contributor - story two.
Email- *artmom@AOl.com*

Pastor Mark A. Willis
MY LIFE GODS GOT PLANS
Pastor- Speaker, Series Contributor- story four.
Email- *m75324509@gmail.com*

April May Diaz
JESUS FOREVER CHANGED MY HEART
Restaurant Owner. Series Contributor- story five.
Kathy Mays Lakeview Café located at 6622 Lakeview Drive, Huntington Beach, California
Email -*Kathymaycafe@gmail.com*

OTHER GOOD WORKS CONTRIBUTORS PAGE

Barbara E. Kompik
I HEAR ANGELS

Author, Speaker, Book Promotor, Series Contributor- story six. Author; Hollyhocks and Roses, *Published 2018.* **Heavens Mist a Mothers Memoir,** *Published 2021.* A Collection of Poetry and Prose by survivors of Abuse, *Published 2022.* **Show Me Your Glory Lord A Mothers Grief for Her Son,** *Published 2022.* Finding My Voices: A Fractured Mind: A Collection: Hope and Healing from Trauma, *Published 2022.* The Therapist Letters (A collection: Offering Hope and Healing from Trauma) *Published 2022.* How's Your Heart Today? **The Dale Kompik Story,** *Published 2023.* The Unstoppable Creative Bipolar Personality, *Published 2023.* Dear Dale: A Tribute to a Friend in Letters and photographs. *Published 2024.* The Bipolar Marriage, Annie and Georges Survival Story, *Published 2024.*
And Many More…
Email- *barbara.e.kompik@gmail.com*

Janice Bobanis
THE BOLD PROCLAIMER

Author, Speaker, Bible-Study Teacher, Series Contributor- story seven.
Author**, In The Beginning Genesis 1-11**, Publisher WestBow Press, Published *2023.*
Email-*janicebobanistcm@gmail.com*

Didier Kwizera
ALWAYS WITH THE LOVE OF JESUS

Missionary Pastor, Church Planter, Contributor- story nine.
Mubara Missionary Church
Email- *didikwiz@gmail.com*

OTHER GOOD WORKS CONTRIBUTORS PAGE

Bonnie McBride
ROSE, HIS GOOD LESSON
Speaker, Series Contributor story eleven.
Email- *lewinerose@gmail.com*

Candy J. Beard
IT ONLY TOOK FIFTEEN YEARS
Author, Award Winning Screenwriter and Producer,
Series Contributor- story twelve.

Films- Vanished - premiered & released on DVD in *2014*.
Cries Unheard & **My Mother's Replacement** - premiered & released on DVD in *2015*. **The Promise** - premiered & released on DVD in *2017*.
A Second Chance - premiered & released on DVD in 2018 But officially got worldwide distribution in August 2024. **The Text** - premiered in June *2022*, released on DVD in Dec. *2023* *But officially got worldwide distribution in July *2024*. Candy has also authored many books and can be located on Amazon and other book retailers.
Email- *candy_dreamscometruefilmsllc@yahoo.com*

Nancy J. Stoll
WHY LORD, WHY
Christ-centered, purpose-oriented speaker, mentor, business owner and advisor. Series contributor-story fourteen.

Author, "**Praise God He Knew I Was a Slow Learner**," Word Smyth Marketing, LLC *2022*. Author of the forthcoming book 2 in the Praise God series, "**Praise God He Knew the Troubles I'd See.**" Founder of The TIARA Club to Success (TIARA Club is acronym for "Through It All Royally Aware Christ Leads Us Boldly") to Success. Business owner and President of Word Smyth Marketing, LLC
Email: *njstoll@gmail.com*

OTHER GOOD WORKS CONTRIBUTORS PAGE

Dawn Hoskins
FROM BROKEN TO BEAUTIFUL

Motivator and Creative Soul Artist, Business Owner, Photographer, Writer, Poet, Designer, Series Contributor-story Sixteen

Owner, **Creative Soul Design.** Layout Designer at **Hope is Now Magazine.** Creative soul Journal available on amazon. Published *2021*

Email: *Dawn@creativesoul.us and dawn@hopeisnowmagazine.com*

SPEAKING TO THE HEART FROM FLICKER TO FLAME BOOK SERIES

Volume Three

✝

*So shall my word be that goes out from my mouth; it shall not return to me empty,
but it shall accomplish that which I purpose, and shall succeed in the thing for which I sent it.*

ISAIAH 55:11

SPEAKING TO THE HEART FROM FLICKER TO FLAME BOOK SERIES

An on-going series of from flicker to Flame Faith Experiences...

If you have a true faith story, you would like to contribute for consideration and possible publication in a future volume, please email at

Speakingtothehearts@gmail.com

For more check out my author page on Amazon
https://www.amazon.com/author/aprilyarber

If you need prayer or would like to pray for others please come join my Facebook group faith family at:
With love April Amanda and Autumn

www.ingramcontent.com/pod-product-compliance
Lightning Source LLC
Chambersburg PA
CBHW072154070526
44585CB00015B/1143